Veneering, Marquetry and Inlay

Veneering, Marquetry and Inlay

The Best Of Fine WoodWorking

The Taunton Press

Cover photo by Vincent Laurence

Taunton
BOOKS & VIDEOS
for fellow enthusiasts

First printing: 1996
Printed in the United States of America

A Fine Woodworking Book

Fine Woodworking® is a trademark of The Taunton Press, Inc.,
registered in the U.S. Patent and Trademark Office.

The Taunton Press, Inc.
63 South Main Street
P.O. Box 5506
Newtown, Connecticut 06470-5506

Library of Congress Cataloging-in-Publication Data

Veneering, marquetry and inlay.
    p. cm. — (The Best of Fine woodworking)
    "A Fine woodworking book" — T.p. verso.
    "23 articles from Fine woodworking magazine" — Introd.
    Includes index.
    ISBN 1-56158-119-4 (pbk.)
    1. Woodwork.   2. Veneers and veneering.   3. Marquetry.
I. Fine woodworking.   II. Series.
TT200.V46   1996
745.51—dc20   95-41543
                                          CIP

Contents

Introduction

Chances are that veneering, marquetry and inlay aren't the very first things we learn as woodworkers. I know that when I began making furniture, these techniques seemed out of reach. I leaned toward simple pieces made from solid wood. Many woodworkers prefer that style, and choose to stay with it. Others, however, want to add another level of detail to their work. Eventually, they may turn to veneering, marquetry or inlay. All three are essential skills for reproducing some period furniture styles. And as the articles in this book will show you, these techniques can produce remarkable results in contemporary furniture. Veneering, in particular, is one of those techniques you tell yourself you don't need to know only until you've tried it. Then you wonder how you managed without it.

In this collection of 23 articles from *Fine Woodworking* magazine, you'll get the best technical advice available in the field. Woodworkers will find information on everything from sawing their own veneers to creating inlay patterns freehand. There's even advice on working materials like birch bark, silver and turquoise. In all, the articles are a great place to start for woodworkers looking to expand their repertoire.

—*Scott Gibson, editor*

The "Best of *Fine Woodworking*" series spans over ten years of *Fine Woodworking* magazine. There is no duplication between these books and the popular *"Fine Woodworking* on..." series. A footnote with each article gives the date of first publication; product availability, suppliers' addresses and prices may have changed since then.

Visiting a Veneer Mill
From steaming logs to thinly sliced sheets

by John Kriegshauser

To begin the veneer-making process, logs that have been sawn into longitudinal halves called flitches are soaked in tanks of boiling water to soften. Then the flitches are hoisted out by a conveyor, and workmen pry off the loose bark with a spud.

Veneer is truly one of the wonders of woodworking—sheets of paper-thin wood, wastelessly sliced from a log by a big knife. The process is easy to understand, but hard to believe. Recently, I had a chance to visit the Pleasant Hill Veneer Co. near Kansas City, Mo. In contrast to giant veneer-making plants that rotary-slice fir and other softwoods for construction plywood, Pleasant Hill is a smaller operation that primarily slices American hardwoods into "face" veneers, which are used by manufacturers to make high-quality sheet goods and cabinet products. During my tour of the mill, the entire veneer-making process was demystified as I watched workers turn raw logs into bundles of perfectly sliced veneer.

The veneer-making process begins at the log yard, where hundreds of magnificent white and red oak, walnut and cherry logs arrive by truck from Iowa, Arkansas and Kansas. Each log has been purchased from a broker, whose initials have been stamped on the butt end of the log. These brokers are independent agents who call on the region's loggers and sawmills searching for suitable veneer logs. Logs are given identifying numbers and stacked in a log yard, where a sprinkler system periodically sprays them with water to prevent them from drying and checking in the hot summer sun. Fred Kyles, the second-shift supervisor, explained that logs left out for four or more weeks are vulnerable to stain from fungal attack; so log inventory has to be turned over quickly.

Sawing and soaking—Each day, Pleasant Hill's 48-in. circular-saw mill cuts enough veneer flitches for a day's slicing. A flitch, in industry parlance, is a slab of the log trimmed to mount on the slicer. First, the sawyer rips the log down the center (the pith), creating a pair of flitches, and then he saws a parallel face down the full length of each. The barky edges remain unsquared for now, for maximum veneer yield. The flitch pairs are then fastened together, heartwood face out, with plastic bands and sent to the soaking tanks. Any bark and sawmill trimmings, as well as the log's waste, are ground into chips and fed into the boiler that supplies power, heat for the dryers and hot water for the soaking tanks.

The soaking tanks are concrete basins about 8 ft. wide, 10 ft. deep and 20 ft. long. Once loaded with flitches, the tanks are filled with scalding water. The soaking process, which lasts one or more days, depending on the species, softens the wood so it will slice cleanly. Soaking tends to even out the wood's color as well. Kyles and I looked on as a workman hoisted off the tank's lid. The water was as black as coffee, and the flitches just poked through its oily, foamy surface. Kyles cautioned me not to fall in.

To ready the flitches for the slicer, the workman fished out a bound pair with a chain hoist and placed it on a conveyor; we could barely see him through the intense steam as he cut the banding and removed the wet bark easily with a spud (see the photo above). He then rolled each flitch to the next workstation. There, one workman trimmed off the checked ends, while another abraded the wood surfaces with an angle-grinder-type rotary planer, to clear away any sand or grit that could damage the slicing knife (see the top photo on p. 10). The journey from tank to slicer takes less than 15 minutes, so the wood remains hot and wet during slicing.

The slicer—As we arrived, the slicer (shown in the bottom photo on p. 10) was being readied for another flitch. Two massive lead screws, which also bear the outfeed conveyer, withdrew the blade carriage, pulling it back on its floor-mounted tracks away from the vertical flitch table. A narrow corridor was created and the slicermen entered it, with the hot flitch dangling from an overhead chain hoist. They pressed the flitch's heartwood face against the table, as a series of small spikes or "dogs," driven by hydraulic pistons, gripped the flitch securely.

Then the machine came to life. The flitch table began moving up and down with increasing speed. The lead screws reversed and pushed the blade carriage forward until the blade almost touched the flitch; then it slowed to an advance that was barely perceptible. By now the flitch was flying up and down 50 times a minute, and the slicermen scurried to their places, opposite one another across the machine's outfeed conveyor. The first slices of veneer were imperfect, falling shy of the full length of the flitch, and the slicer-men hurriedly tossed them onto the floor. As the first full slices came off, the two men faced one another and worked in perfect unison to stack the sheets in the same order they came off the flitch.

At this point, Sam Clark, Pleasant Hill's production manager and millwright, pointed out some of the finer points of veneer slicing. "The flitch table," he said, "does not merely go up and down; the tracks it rides on are angled at about a 20°, creating a slightly diagonal cut to produce the smoothest veneer surface." Blue stain, a problem wherever steel meets wet, acidic wood, is controlled by limiting the wood's contact with the knife. A cam mechanism, called the offset, tilts the knife carriage *away* from the flitch at the end of each down stroke so no contact is made on the up stroke. The action of the offset is so subtle that I would have missed it had Clark not pointed it out. Another anti-stain measure is an electric heating element in the knife mounting that warms the blade, drying it between slices.

Clark also explained that large-volume buyers that manufacture plywood and other veneered products require veneer that's highly uniform in thickness. To ensure this uniformity, the blade carriage must advance precisely the same amount for each slice. This is accomplished with a pawl-and-gear mechanism that advances one notch for each slicing stroke, like a giant clock mechanism. The axle of this gear wheel is the lead screw that advances the knife carriage. The gap between the blade and pressure bar also regulates the veneer thickness. However, this gap is set to a bit less than the finished dimension of the veneer. This way, the wood, which in the context of the enormous forces of the slicer is soft and spongy, compresses as it is sliced, producing the smoothest surfaces.

When the big slicer finally stopped, the carriage was withdrawn and the remainder of the flitch, still almost 4 in. thick, was hoisted onto a dolly and taken to a large motorized saw that rides on a track above the flitch. This saw split the flitch right down its pith, and the two pieces were then remounted on a second, smaller slicer. Kyles told me that slicing a full-size flitch any further results in veneer with excessive tearout. "So we split the flitch and slice each half separately on the smaller slicer, flipping it end for end so we're always cutting from the center out toward the sapwood." Kyles showed me one of the split flitches sliced earlier on the second machine, and indeed, the quartersawn grain was clean and perfect.

Drying and trimming—Once sliced, the veneer is promptly taken to the dryer: an enormous, 40-ft.-long sheet-metal box. At the entry end, two workers load the flitch sheet by sheet onto a conveyor made of stainless-steel mesh. Just inside the dryer, a second conveyor descends from above to keep the veneer flat during its three-minute journey. The interior of the dryer consists of five enormous, rotating drums. The conveyor first goes under one drum and then over the next, as a battery of fans blows heated air across the exposed faces. When the veneer reaches the other end, workers restack the sheets, keeping them in consecutive order.

If the veneers are destined for a North American customer, they are usually crated and readied for shipment. But if they're for the European market, the flitches are first edge trimmed, and any end-checking or stain is trimmed away. (Veneer is a competitive industry; no one wants to pay to haul trimmings across the Atlantic.) The trimming is performed on a stout, iron machine called a clipper. The clipper's 16-ft. blade and the hydraulic cylinders that drive it are concealed in a housing suspended above the worktable. The worker positions a stack of veneer under a laser light that identifies the line of cut. Once the worker is satisfied with the position, the machine is switched on and the blade chops off the waste.

Sharpening a 16-ft.-long knife

"Smoothly cut, tearout-free veneer is what the customer wants," Fred Kyles, of Pleasant Hill Veneer, explained. "The art to the process is in how you soak the wood and in how you sharpen the knife." With that, Fred led me into an outbuilding just large enough to hold a giant sharpening machine and a honing bench.

The heavy, 16-ft.-long veneer-slicing knives, which are resharpened every day, are moved to and from the sharpening shed via a chain hoist and overhead track. Once there, each knife is securely bolted onto the grinding machine. The grinder, shown at right, tracks slowly along the length of the knife, bathed in a continuous shower of coolant, producing a flat, rather than hollow, grind on the knife's edge. Next, the knife is transferred to the honing bench, where it is mounted edge up. Kyles then demonstrated how the wire edge is removed: He reached into a coffee can full of kerosene and pulled out two carborundum stones, one for each hand. As Kyles walked the length of the blade, he worked the stones with a circular motion; one stone honed the knife's bevel, while the other honed its flat side. Final honing was done with hard Arkansas stones, which left a polished edge. It was terrifying to watch Kyles reach across that giant razor-sharp blade. Over the years, he confessed, he had received many serious cuts, but all had healed with only faint scars.

In spite of every precaution to keep the knife from prematurely dulling, once in a while it gets nicked and production must stop; a nicked knife causes a small but conspicuous cross-grain tear in the veneer that's almost impossible to sand out after the veneer has been glued down. Millwright Sam Clark showed us how he burnishes the crumpled steel back into place and hones out the remaining nick by hand with an Arkansas stone while the knife is still mounted in the slicer. The slicermen can usually detect nails or barbed wire embedded in the log by a telltale blue stain appearing in the veneer. But what about bullets? "A lead slug is no problem," Kyles assured me. "The knife will cut right through it. But a copper-jacketed 30-06, that's a problem. All you can do is hope to find the entry hole before you hit that bullet." —*J.K.*

The veneer slicer's 16-ft.-long blade must be sharpened every day of use. First, the special knife grinder shown here regrinds the edge as the machine travels along huge, precise guide rails. Then the blade is honed using two hand-held slip stones.

To prepare the log flitches for slicing, the rough ends are cut off with an automated chainsaw. Then any remaining bark, dirt or surface debris that might later nick the veneer-slicing knife is removed with a hand-held rotary planer.

Pleasant Hill Veneer Co.'s big slicing machine effortlessly moves a 12-ft.-long oak flitch past the machine's stationary knife 50 times a minute. The sheets of veneer that peel off come down a conveyor and are stacked by the workmen in consecutive order.

Instead of a simple guillotine-drop action, the blade makes a "sine wave" cut: First the left corner of the blade plunges through the flitch, and then as the right corner begins to drop, the left ascends. The blade rolls through the veneer with a rhythmic motion, producing a clean, perfect cut.

Now the trimmed veneer flitches are passed under a special scanner that assesses the surface area of the flitch; this information is fed to a computer that multiplies the surface area by the number of veneer sheets in the flitch to obtain the official tally in square feet. Finally, Kyles led me to the warehouse where pallets of veneer awaited the inspection of haggling veneer buyers, the majority of whom were from Europe. He removed a cardboard dust-cover from a nearby pallet of white oak and called my attention to the veneer's even color and smooth surface. "That's as fine a slicing job as you'll find anywhere in the world," he said proudly.

As I was leaving, Steve Kingston, vice president of the mill, explained to me why Pleasant Hill's British parent company, Union Veneers, is currently expanding the mill's facilities. "Many species, like teak, will fade from fashion as their scarcity drives their price up. But the white oak forests of North America are expanding," he said. He went on to explain why, in his opinion, the veneer industry is environmentally sound. "We selectively harvest the few, large, mature trees in a tract of forest, allowing the newer growth a chance for some sunlight. Since each log yields a great deal of veneer, the process can go on indefinitely." □

John Kriegshauser is a furniture designer/craftsman and shop director in the College of Architecture at the Illinois Institute of Technology in Chicago, Ill. Bruce Best, an architectural designer with AGMP in Lee's Summit, Mo., assisted in writing this article.

Figured veneers
by Jim Dumas

Although many wood species are available as plainsawn or quartersawn lumber, that's just the tip of the iceberg when it comes to the vast range of grain figures available in veneers. Part of the reason for this variety is the high degree of control the veneer mill has in the way a log is sliced. Some grain figures are revealed or enhanced by being sliced in a particular way. For example, rotary-slicing bird's-eye maple creates the most round, perfect eye figure. Woodworkers aiming to add a distinguished look to their work, or elevate a project's overall appearance and value, often want unusually figured or exotic veneers. But they don't always know what to ask for; sometimes the trade names of

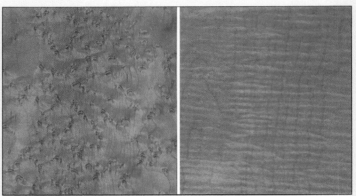

Bird's-eye (left)—The name itself describes it best. Once considered a defect, the best bird's-eye flitches are now expensive and in demand. These veneers are most often rotary cut or half-round sliced (in an arc) to produce the most uniform distribution of nice round eyes. Bird's-eye is most common in maple (shown), but bird's-eye does rarely occur in a few other species.

Curly (right)—Contortions in grain direction that reflect light differently create an appearance of undulating waves known as curly grain. Many species develop this figure, but most commonly maple, shown. Stump and butt sections of trees often produce a diagonal, staircase-like curl referred to as "angel steps," and a rolling curl figure that is called "cross-fire."

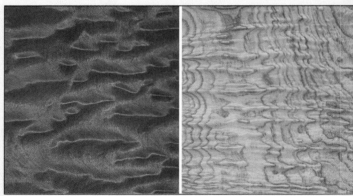

Quilted (left)—Although greatly resembling a larger and exaggerated version of pommele or blister figure, quilted figure has bulges that are elongated and closely crowded. Quilted grain looks veritably three-dimensional when seen at its billowy best. It's most commonly found in mahogany, moabi (shown), maple, sapele and myrtle, and occurs only rarely in other species.

Peanut shell (right)—When certain woods exhibit a quilted or blistered figure, they are rotary cut to promote a random, wild grain pattern as well. This peanut-shell grain creates a visual illusion similar to quilted figure: the veneer appears bumpy and pitted, when in fact it's flat. Tamo (Japanese ash), shown, and bubinga are the two most popular examples of this figure.

special veneers can be confusing. This is more of a problem when mail-ordering veneer because you can't see what you're getting before you buy it.

The illustrations of distinctively figured veneers shown in the photos below are intended to acquaint would-be veneer buyers with some of the more common trade names for some conventional veneer figures. However, the names I've given in the captions aren't necessarily universal for two reasons: First, simple names for a few common figure types are barely sufficient to cover all the possible examples of figure in any species of veneer. Every tree grows a little differently, and within a single flitch, you often find an entire range of figures. Second, veneer-figure nomenclature varies from country to country, and is even different among veneer sellers and users in different regions. I've

seen plenty of veneer sold under the "wrong" name—wrong simply because it disagrees with my own veneer vernacular. In addition to the names listed and discussed here, there are some very unusual figure names, such as pippy (looks like measles), drapé (looks like draping vines) and plum pudding (looks like elongated dark plums). Other figures include roe, rippling and finger roll. More names come up now and then, and on a few occasions, I've even had to coin a new name for a veneer figure that defied classification. □

Jim Dumas is the owner of Certainly Wood/Hardwood Veneer and Lumber Co., a supplier of veneers to studios and contract shops, in East Aurora, N.Y. Wood samples courtesy of Certainly Wood.

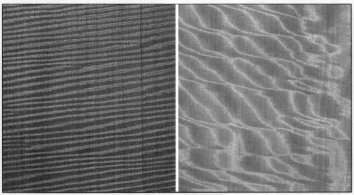

Fiddleback *(left)—An estimable variation of curly figure, this figure's name is taken from its customary use for violin backs. Logs for fiddleback veneers are quartersawn to produce very straight grain with nearly perpendicular curls running uninterrupted from edge to edge. Maple, makore (shown), anegre and English sycamore head a list of about 12 fiddleback-prone species.*

Mottled *(right)—Wavy grain combines with spiral, interlocked grain to produce a wrinkled, blotchy figure known as mottle. The mottled figure may be scattered randomly (broken mottle), or appear as a regular checkerboard pattern (block mottle). Members of the mahogany family, koa, sapele, bubinga and African satinwood, shown, most commonly exhibit mottled figure.*

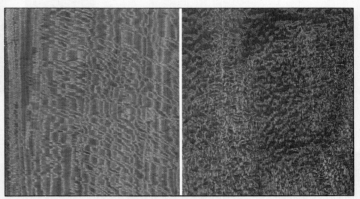

Bee's wing *(left)—Smaller, tighter and more intense than mottled figure, although structurally similar, bee's-wing figure is said to resemble that insect's appendage when magnified. (I haven't actually compared them.) East Indian satinwood, shown, is extremely well known for having this figure, and it also occurs occasionally in narra, mahogany and eucalyptus.*

Pommele *(right)—This figure resembles a puddle surface during a light rain: a dense pattern of small rings enveloping one another. Some say this has a "suede" or "furry" look. It's usually found in extremely large trees of African species like sapele (shown), bubinga and makore. Some domestic species with a sparser, larger figure are referred to as "blistered."*

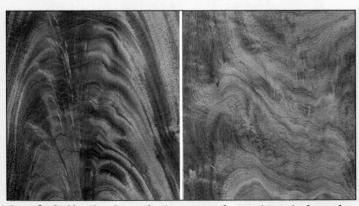

Crotch *(left)—Cut from the juncture of a tree's main branches and trunk, crotch figures are often subcategorized as flame, plume, roostertail, feather or burning bush. All of these descriptive terms serve to convey the range of this figure's appearance. Seldom found in large sizes, mahogany (shown) and walnut species dominate the field of crotch veneers.*

Swirl *(right)—This figure is a visually gentler version of regular crotch figure. As the name implies, the grain meanders and swirls around, often seeming to convolute and fold in upon itself. The densest portions of the swirl show up darker or shaded compared to the lighter surrounding wood. Swirl occurs in species including walnut (shown), mahogany, cherry and maple.*

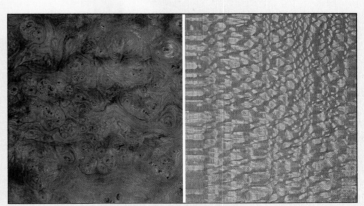

Burls *(left)—Growths on trees produce some of the most prized veneers. Usually available in smallish, often defective sheets, burls feature swirling grain around clusters of dormant buds, rings or eyes. Varieties include "cluster burl" or "cat's paw burl." Redwood, oak, ash, madrone, elm (shown) and walnut are common burl species; exotic burls include mappa, thuya and imboya.*

Button *(right)—When woods with large medullary rays are quartersawn, the harder, shinier rays are more fully exhibited and show up as "snowflakes" or buttons on a straight-grained background. Some veneer species, such as white oak, lacewood (shown) and American sycamore, are more attractive when sliced to reveal this button figure.*

Practice pays off. *The author so admired a sunburst veneer match he ordered from a local supplier that he taught himself how to make his own. It took some practice, but now he can make patterns like this tabletop in crotch mahogany.*

From *Fine Woodworking* (March 1995) 111:40-44

Veneer Matching:
From Small Sheets, Great Patterns

How to make the best possible use of extraordinary veneers

by Frank Pollaro

There was a time when I couldn't imagine using veneer for anything more than covering the raw edges on plywood. Then a special table came along. I thought it might be nice to do something besides my usual solid-wood glue-up with an occasional inlay.

I had a local veneer supplier make an ebony sunburst for the tabletop. When the top arrived, I felt such admiration for the craftsman who had so perfectly arranged those 20 pieces of ebony veneer into a brilliant star. But besides admiration, I was determined to do the veneer work myself next time.

After ordering some veneer and reading up on veneering, I began cutting, arranging and pressing some basic veneer matches. Two years and several hundred square feet of veneer later, I cut my first 16-piece sunburst match for a tabletop. It turned out beautifully, but it did take some time.

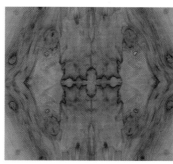

BOOK-MATCH

DIAMOND MATCH

FOUR-PIECE MATCH

REVERSE-DIAMOND MATCH

Four simple matches make the most of smaller leaves of veneer. A book-match works best with veneers that have asymmetrical grain or figure patterns because the match creates symmetry. For the same reason, a four-piece match is best-suited for burls and other similarly wild-figured veneers. Diamond and reverse-diamond matches are most impressive with straight-grained veneers.

I usually pick an obvious mark, like a swirl, pin knot or area of particularly remarkable grain, and keep this mark the same distance from the edge of each leaf of veneer. That way, a pattern looks balanced or symmetrical throughout a match, regardless of whether it's a simple book-match or the most complex sunburst.

Book-matches and four-piece matches

A book-match is when two leaves of veneer are opened from a common edge, as you would open a book (see the top left photo). Book-matching is best done with veneers that are obviously asymmetrical: Two veneer leaves opened so they look like mirror images of each other form a symmetrical, balanced whole.

When four leaves of veneer are book-matched and then book-matched again, perpendicular to the first seam, the result is called a four-piece

Since then, I've worked increasingly with veneers and done many sunburst matches as well as plenty of simpler matches. I've learned a few things in the course of this work that make veneer matching easier and the results more consistently successful. You don't have to tackle anything complicated to enjoy veneering. The figure, color and diversity of the veneers that are now available is breathtaking. Here are some techniques that have helped me.

The basic principle

The eye doesn't notice the precise width of a sheet, or leaf, of veneer, but the eye will notice sloppy asymmetry or poorly matched grain lines. That's why it's more important to make sure the grain lines in a pattern meet cleanly or are aligned in an attractive manner than it is to have all of the pieces of a pattern exactly the same size. This is the secret to a successful veneer match.

match (see the top right photo above). Burls and odd patterns commonly are used for a book- or four-piece match.

Diamond and reverse-diamond matches

The most sophisticated matches commonly used for square shapes are the diamond and reverse diamond. These are best-suited for straight-grained or striped woods. For a diamond match, the grain is positioned parallel to the four outside edges of the square (see the bottom left photo). For a reverse diamond, the grain is perpendicular to the outside edges (see the bottom right photo).

Creating a diamond or reverse diamond match is not an obvious process like a book- or four-piece match. For either the diamond or reverse diamond, I begin by cutting the four component pieces, each slightly longer than a finished side of the match and slightly wider than half of the match. I cut angles at 45° to the grain on two

Fig. 1: Creating a diamond or reverse-diamond

The cutting and taping sequence is the same for diamond and reverse-diamond matches. The only difference is that the grain is oriented perpendicularly to the outside edges for a reverse diamond (below left) and parallel to the outside edges for a diamond (below right). Mark individual leaves as shown.

Reverse-diamond match

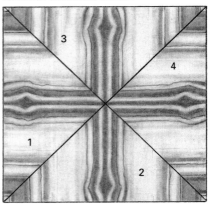

Diamond match

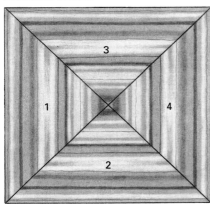

Step 1
First cut opposing leaves from their midpoints to the opposite corners.

Step 2
Now lay the cut half of #1 over #2. Align grain as well as you can, and then mark and cut #2. Tape these two pieces together. Repeat steps 1 and 2 with pieces #3 and #4.

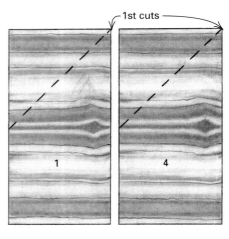

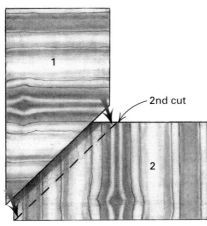

1st cuts

2nd cut

Step 3
Cut diagonally across L-shaped piece to create a right triangle. This is one-half of the match.

3rd cut

Waste

Step 4
Lay section #1-2 over section #3-4. Mark and cut as in step 3. Tape the two halves together, and you're done.

4th cut

Waste

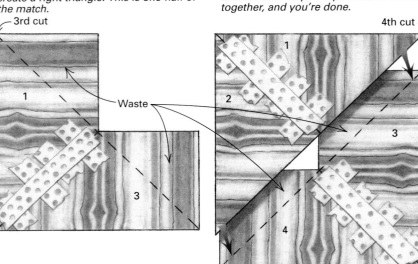

Fig. 2: Laying out a sunburst

By positioning veneer leaves as shown, you can eliminate any abrupt changes in figure between leaves. This will keep the pattern looking more balanced throughout.

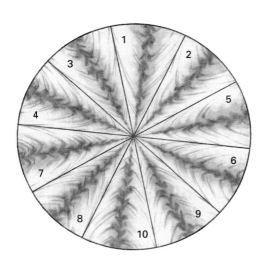

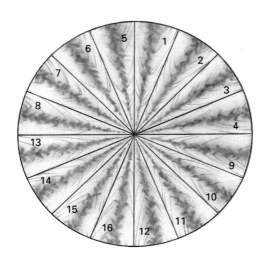

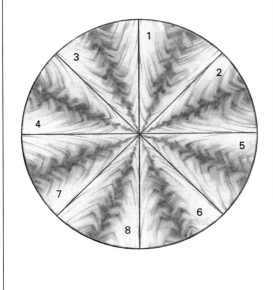

Drawings: Michael Gellatly

of the four pieces from the center of a long side to an opposite corner (see step 1 in figure 1).

Then I place one of the cut quarters over another uncut piece of veneer (this will be the quarter adjacent to it), carefully aligning the two pieces to get a 90° corner (step 2). I mark the second piece with a sharp pencil, cut it using a veneer saw and a good straightedge and then tape the two pieces together with veneer tape. I repeat the process with the other two pieces.

What I have now are two L-shaped pieces. I draw a line diagonally across the corners and then cut along that line, leaving a right triangle that is half of the match (step 3). This half is then laid over the other, grain lines are aligned and the bottom piece is marked and cut to form the second half of the square. Finally, the two halves are taped together to complete the match (step 4).

The sunburst match

By far the most beautiful of all matches is the sunburst (see the photo on p. 12). It is most often used for round tables, but it also works well for squares, ovals, quarter- and half-rounds and arcs, which make beautiful headboards for beds.

Laying out, cutting and arranging the wedges—To make a sunburst match, I determine how many leaves of veneer I need. For the best results, they must be sequential leaves. That is, the leaves must be in the same order as they were sliced off the log, so grain variations are subtle and occur only gradually with each successive leaf in a stack, or book, as it's called. I usually make sunbursts using eight, 10, 16, 20 or 32 leaves (see figure 2).

I decide how many leaves I need by multiplying the diameter of the desired circle by *pi* (3.14 is close enough) and then dividing this number by the width of my veneers. For example, for a round table, 30 in. dia., I'd multiply 30 in. by 3.14 and divide that number by the width of my veneers (say, 7 in.). In this case, the number of leaves I'd need to complete the circle is about 13½. I can't round the number down; therefore, I aim for 16 leaves because I have made 16-piece matches before, so I have a template to speed layout.

The templates are simple to make: For eight-, 16- and 32-piece matches, I halve a circle, halve the half and so on. I make the template just slightly wider (¹⁄₁₆ in. is about right) than the exact angle of each piece so that when half of the circle is assembled, I'll have slightly more than half of a sunburst. That way, I can tape up the two halves separately, and then trim each half with a straightedge. The two halves can be joined to form a complete circle. But I'm getting ahead of myself.

After I've established the number of leaves in my sunburst and made a template, I number each leaf in sequence. I preview what the finished sunburst will look like when it's assembled, so I know where to cut the individual sheets of veneer. I do this by taping

LAYING OUT THE TOP

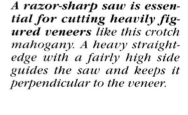

Preview a whole sunburst on one leaf of veneer. By using a pair of hinged mirrors (duct tape will hold them together), the author can see how a sunburst will look before the first leaf has been cut.

A razor-sharp saw is essential for cutting heavily figured veneers like this crotch mahogany. A heavy straightedge with a fairly high side guides the saw and keeps it perpendicular to the veneer.

A template reduces layout time while improving accuracy. Even if you're only planning to do one sunburst, the time spent making a template will be well worth the effort.

two pieces of mirror together to create an adjustable angle, which I set on edge on one leaf in the match. By adjusting the angle to match the template and then moving the mirrors around, I can see the whole match before I make the first cut (see the top photo). I can be sure to get exactly the effect I'm looking for.

When I like what I see, I double-check that the space between the mirrors corresponds to the template, and then I trace along the inside edges of both mirrors. The next step is to cut one edge of this piece, using a reliable straightedge and a freshly sharpened veneer saw (see the center photo on this page). I now have a leaf of veneer with only one side of the wedge-shaped section cut. I lay this leaf on each of the remaining leaves and mark along the cut edge. This ensures that each section will be taken from the

CUTTING, TAPING A SUNBURST MATCH

Tape across the seams every 5 to 6 in. and then all the way along the seams. Stop just shy of the center, so you can see where all the points come together. Paper veneer tape scrapes off easily after the veneer is bonded to the substrate. And it won't tear the veneer fibers like other kinds of tape.

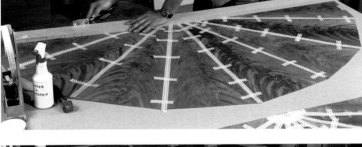

Careful trimming with a veneer saw yields a perfect half-circle. The author sizes his templates, so half the match is slightly larger than a half-circle This allows him to trim thin wedges off each side and not have to worry about the two halves of the match falling short of making a full circle.

Rolling the tape with a veneer roller helps achieve a flat pressing. Make sure the edge of one leaf doesn't overlap an adjacent leaf. This prevents edges from breaking off in the press or a veneer leaf not adhering because it wasn't touching the substrate.

p. 14). The improvement may be subtle, but it's worth doing.

With the sequence established, the last decision I need to make is whether I want a pinwheel or a book-matched sunburst. In a pinwheel sunburst, the leaves are arranged with all the same faces up, and the resulting pattern looks like, well, a pinwheel. In a book-match sunburst, alternate leaves are flipped to create a running book-match. I lay out a sunburst both ways before I decide.

Taping and preparing the sunburst for the press— I tape the wedge-shaped sections across the seams every 5 to 6 in. and then over most of the length of the seam. To align the sections, I stop taping just shy of the center so that I can see where all the points come together (see the top two photos at left).

I assemble the two halves of the match separately. Then I lay a straightedge across the edge of the first half so that the straightedge just touches where the points of veneer converge, and there's an even wedge of veneer to cut off to the left and right of center. There should be about ¼ in. on both sides at the perimeter of the half-circle. I trim carefully (see the photo at left) because thin strips are prone to tearout. Then I repeat for the other half. I tape the two halves together, being particularly careful to line up the centers of the two halves. The match is complete (see the bottom photo).

The sunburst should be pressed to the substrate as quickly as possible, particularly when using figured veneers such as crotch mahogany. These figured veneers tend to dry out unevenly, causing them to lift in places and making them difficult to press. If you can't get the match in the press the same day that you assemble it, make sure you cover the match with plastic (garbage bags work great for this), and weight it heavily.

If the sunburst is lifting off the table in the middle when it's uncovered, spray a light mist of water with a little glycerin (I dilute the glycerin 10 to one) near the outside edge. Allow the match to flatten for a few minutes before pressing. If the sunburst is lifting around the edges, spray the middle area, which will help prevent it from cracking once in the press. When I do press the sunburst, I make sure I also press a piece of backing veneer on the opposite side of the substrate. This equalizes the forces of wood movement and ensures the tabletop will stay flat. The backing veneer need not be the same highly figured wood. □

same place in each leaf, so I get the same effect I saw in the mirror. When all the leaves are marked, I cut along the marked lines. Now I take the template, mark the second side of the angle onto each of the pieces and cut them.

The next step is crucial, but not at all intuitive. If the leaves are laid out in sequence (one to 16, for example), then number one would be right next to number 16. With that layout, changes in the figure from leaf one to leaf 16 could be subtle or glaringly obvious. A knot might pierce a stack of veneer leaves at an angle, and the resulting sunburst would look as though it spiraled, an asymmetrical, not very pleasing effect.

To make the sunburst appear more balanced, I take the leaves out of chronological order and then assemble them in a sequence that eliminates any huge jump between leaves (see figure 2 on

Frank Pollaro teaches workshops on veneering and is a designer and builder of fine furniture in East Orange, N.J.

Visual Tricks with Veneers

Ultra-thin layer reveals hidden inlays

by Tom Duffy

Some years back, I accidentally picked up two photo transparencies of the same piece of furniture and held them to the light with the images superimposed. I was shocked that I could "see through" a piece of furniture, and the design possibilities got me thinking about ways to make wood transparent. I have always been very keen on the light-reflective properties of wood: the way wood changes color and luster when viewed from various angles or under different lighting conditions. I eventually realized that wood's translucency is an extension of those light-reflective qualities. This all sounds rational and measured, but I must admit that a mistake actually revealed the possibilities to me. Anyone who has worked with veneer has probably experienced, at one time or another, the sinking feeling after sanding through the veneer. It was in this serendipitous error that I found the means to incorporate transparent screens of wood in my designs.

The idea of a screened image has particular appeal to me because it makes invention and deceit possible. As in the image of a person walking in the fog or in the characters half-hidden behind translucent curtains in Jean Genet's play, *The Screens*, a reduction of the image evokes our curiosity. The system I developed uses a double layer of veneers; the base layer, inlaid with a design, is covered by a second layer of veneer, which is also usually inlaid. Then by carefully sanding the cover layer until it is only a few thousandths of an inch thick, I reveal the hidden images of the base layer. I didn't know how to describe my techniques for screening images with veneers until I adopted the expression "pentimento." Lillian Hellman's book, *Pentimento*, describes it as follows.

"Old paint on canvas, as it ages, sometimes becomes transparent. When that happens it is possible, in some pictures, to see the original lines: a tree will show through a woman's dress, a child makes way for a dog, a large boat is no longer on an open sea. That is called pentimento because the painter 'repented,' changed his mind. Perhaps it would be as well to say that the old conception, replaced by a later choice, is a way of seeing and then seeing again." (From *Pentimento: A Book of Portraits* by Lillian Hellman, copyright ©1973 by Lillian Hellman. By permission of Little, Brown and Co.)

Bi-level designs—Designing a pentimento panel is a challenge because the design is created on two levels that must work together. Some interesting effects can be achieved by having lines begin on the base layer and terminate on the cover layer, as can be seen in the folding screen at right. Here the design not only flows across the panels, but also between the two layers.

After experimenting with various materials, I've concluded that the pentimento is most effective when the grain patterns and colors of two veneer layers are as closely matched as possible. I first tried inlaying designs into birch-veneer plywood and

Photo: Koshen

Duffy was attracted to screened images because they add mystery to a piece. His folding screen is made of laminated double layers of holly veneer. He sanded back the cover veneer to reveal inlays in the base layer and created a translucent effect that he calls pentimento.

then laminating a cover layer of holly, but I found that the different grain patterns and colors created a confusion or "static," which detracted from the overall effect. While you're probably familiar with book-matching and slip-matching veneers, I use what I call drop-matching to eliminate much of this static. I overlay "sister" pieces, consecutive sheets of veneer from the same flitch, aligning the grain of the two layers as closely as possible. My favorite veneer is holly because its color and grain let the base-layer designs show through, and it provides a good background for the inlays in the cover layer. When selecting veneers for inlays, keep in mind that the brighter primary colors work well in the base layer since they will be screened. To preview the effect of a particular base inlay, I've devised a "screen" using two or three layers of waxed paper. Laying this screen on a veneer will fairly accurately show how the base will look through varying thicknesses of the covering holly, as shown in the photo below.

The techniques—The first step in creating a pentimento panel is to make a single drawing on frosted acetate (available from art-supply stores), which will show the design for both layers of veneer. Draw each layer's design in a different color to simplify pattern development and to make it easier when you transfer the designs to the veneers. Also, reference the acetate to the sister sheets of veneer so you can reposition the veneers and precisely align each design layer. Now, transfer the design to the veneer with carbon paper or by placing the acetate under the veneer on a light table.

With the design phase completed, I laminated the base layer of holly veneer to a stable core, such as plywood or medium-density fiberboard (MDF). I rolled a very thin, uniform layer of white glue on the core with a printer's brayer, a 3½-in.-wide hard-foam hand roller used for inking printing plates (available from Art Supplies Wholesale, 4 Enon St., Beverly, Mass. 01915; 508-922-2420). Be sure

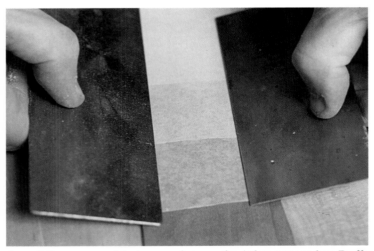

A multilayer waxed-paper mask over the inlay veneer lets Duffy preview how the inlays will look as the top layer is sanded off.

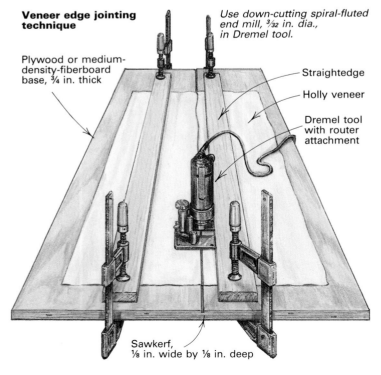

Veneer edge jointing technique

Use down-cutting spiral-fluted end mill, ³⁄₃₂ in. dia., in Dremel tool.

Plywood or medium-density-fiberboard base, ¾ in. thick

Straightedge

Holly veneer

Dremel tool with router attachment

Sawkerf, ⅛ in. wide by ⅛ in. deep

to use a clear-drying white glue because a yellow glue will, in effect, add a yellow lens to the composition. I used Weldbond Universal Space Age Bonding Adhesive that I bought at my local hardware store. A vacuum veneer press, made from a converted photographic printing press, provides a quick and easy way to laminate veneered panels. The thick glass platen provides a flat surface impervious to glue, and the heavy black bladder applies uniform pressure over the entire piece so that just a few pieces of masking tape will hold the veneer in position. A thin layer of packing foam protects the bladder from squeeze-out, and the foam won't stick to the wood. I left the panel in the press for five to six hours because the lack of air in the vacuum extends the glue's setting time.

If I'm veneering large panels, I will also laminate the reverse side with a backing veneer to avoid warping, but I've found this step unnecessary for panels less than about a square foot and for molded shapes. Also, larger panels generally require you to butt-join sheets of veneer to cover a side. I've developed an edge jointing technique, using my Dremel-tool router attachment, for producing perfect butt joints with very little waste. (The router attachment is available from Dremel, 4915 21st St., Racine, Wisc. 53406.) As shown in the drawing, you will need a base of ¾-in.-thick plywood or MDF, about 2 ft. wide and at least as long as the veneer. Rip a ⅛-in.-deep sawkerf centered down the length of the base, and then butt the veneers together on the base so that the joint is centered over the sawkerf. Secure one sheet of veneer by positioning and clamping a straightedge, slightly longer than the veneer, so that a ³⁄₃₂-in.-dia. end mill mounted in the Dremel tool can be guided down the center of the sawkerf. Secure the second sheet of veneer in the same manner, positioning and clamping another straightedge as close to the sawkerf as possible without interfering with the Dremel tool. Then run the router the length of the jig, trimming both veneers simultaneously. A down-cutting spiral-fluted end mill gives a very clean cut and the cutting action holds the veneer to the base. (For your local distributor of these end mills, contact Bassett Rotary Tool Co., 710 W. Fisher St., Monticello, Ind. 47960; 219-583-7166.) Usually one pass will mate the edges perfectly, but if necessary, butt the veneers together again and repeat this procedure.

Most of my pentimento designs are inlaid lines, dots and squares, as shown on the previous page, that I cut from dyed wood veneers. I use a variety of inlaying techniques depending on the shape of the inlay. I slice thin strips of veneer with an Ulmia double-knife inlay cutter (available from Lee Valley Tools, 1080 Morrison Drive, Ottawa, Ont., Canada K2H 8K7; 613-596-0350) and rout the grooves to receive them with an appropriate size, down-cutting spiral-fluted end mill in a variable-speed Dremel Moto-tool with a router-base attachment. For small dots, I made a veneer punch, as shown in the top photo on the facing page, to match the end mill I use for boring the holes. To make the punch, I drilled a ¹⁄₁₆-in.-dia. by ½-in.-deep hole into the end of a piece of ³⁄₈-in.-dia. by 3-in.-long tool steel and ground it to a sharp edge. Then at the other end, I drilled a ⅛-in.-dia. clearance hole to meet the previously drilled hole. I heat-treated both ends of the punch so that it would hold an edge and not mushroom over when hit with a hammer. After destroying many dots that got jammed up in the end of the punch, I've found that three is about the maximum you can safely punch out before stopping to push them through with the blunt end of a ¹⁄₁₆-in.-dia. drill bit. For larger dots, I secured the veneer to a pine backing board with double-faced tape and drilled out the dots with a ½-in.-dia. plug cutter in a drill press. The matching holes were drilled with a Forstner bit.

Squares and odd-shaped inlays were first cut out with an X-Acto knife or chopped with a chisel. I used double-faced tape to hold the inlay in position on the background veneer as I scribed around the inlay with the knife. Once you have done this, remove the inlay, but leave the excess double-faced tape on the background veneer. The tape makes delicate excavations more visible and it protects the background veneer from the adhesive you'll use later to secure the inlay. Now, score the line more deeply, this time with the handle of the knife tipped toward the center of the pattern to offset the bevel of the blade and to create a vertical cut. Then excavate the waste to about $\frac{1}{16}$ in. of the score line with a down-cutting router bit in the Dremel tool. I've found that slowing the Dremel tool down to about 10,000 RPM allows better chip clearance and also significantly increases the life of the bit. Rescoring with your X-Acto knife will remove the last of the waste; then test and trim for a perfect fit.

I glued the inlays in the veneer with a five-minute epoxy, applying it to the void with an awl, as shown in the center photo. Because the epoxy is 100% solids, it won't shrink the veneer and leave gaps, which might happen if you use contact cement or water-base glues. Position the inlay and tap it into place with the butt end of your knife. If the inlay won't stay in place, secure it with clear tape. Once the epoxy has set, remove any clear tape, as well as the double-faced tape. If these tapes are left in place too long, they will leave black smudges that must be removed with mineral spirits. After completing the inlaid design of the base veneer, I used a sharp scraper to clean up the epoxy, making every stroke from a different angle to avoid chatter marks. Don't try for perfection when scraping or you will hollow out the soft veneer around the hard epoxy—a defect that usually doesn't show up until you apply a finish. After scraping I sanded the base veneer with a large thick-plastic platen and a full sheet of 120-grit paper until the surface was smooth and flat.

The second layer—The sister sheet of holly is now veneered over the base layer and is aligned with the previously drawn reference marks. The designs and patterns are then inlaid into the cover veneer the same as they were into the base layer, but with one exception. When inlaying these designs, it is best to go through the cover layer and into the base layer. This way the lines stay clean and crisp when the cover veneer is sanded to about 0.004-in. thickness.

Now with all the inlays in place, scrape and sand, again with a large thick-plastic platen and a full sheet of 120-grit paper. As sanding continues, the images of the inlays in the base layer start to "ghost" through, as seen in the bottom photo. With more sanding, the colors become more vivid and the base images become clearer. Continue sanding until you have almost achieved the desired screen and surface smoothness, and then change to 220-grit followed by 280-grit paper to remove sanding scratches. Although you might be tempted to speed things up with a belt sander, I strongly suggest you resist the urge: it's far too easy to sand right through your cover layer.

At this moment, the pentimento has the most appeal to me; it is "in-the-white," straight from the sandpaper. Unfortunately, you must seal and finish the panel. I send my pieces out for a sprayed finish of 40 to 60 coats of water-white lacquer. I think the resulting high-gloss finish really accentuates the detailing of the pentimento work. I avoid varnishes because they tend to yellow holly very quickly. For finishing in the home shop, you might want to try Hydrocote, a water-base non-toxic lacquer (available from Highland Hardware, 1045 N. Highland Ave., Atlanta, Ga. 30306; 800-241-6748). Although milky white in color, Hydrocote dries as transparently as nitrocellulose lacquer, and it can be sprayed on, with conventional or low-pressure systems, or brushed on. For more on Hydrocote, see *FWW* #69, p. 80.

The folding screen displayed my veneered images just as I had hoped. When people see my screen, most of them walk around to see the other side, thinking it is translucent. To me, this is proof that what I set out to do has been accomplished. □

Tom Duffy is an Ogdensburg, N.Y., woodworker and furnituremaker.

This shopmade punch makes easy work of popping out $\frac{1}{16}$-in.-dia. veneer dots for inlaying into the author's pentimento designs.

Above: *When inlaying small strips or dots, the author controls the amount of epoxy he uses by applying it with a fine-point awl. He then taps the inlay into place with the butt end of an X-Acto knife.* ***Below:*** *Although it is tempting to use a belt sander to finish up a panel, hand-sanding with a large flat block and a full sheet of paper provides much greater control and ensures a flat surface with no dips or gouges.*

Using Shop-Sawn Veneer

Cut thick with the bandsaw, it works like solid wood, stays put like plywood

by Paul Harrell

Sideboard squeezed from a small plank— *By doing his own sawing, the author coaxed the primary veneer and edging for this sideboard from a single plank of jarrah. The legs, stretchers and lighter veneer are mahogany.*

I recently came upon a beautiful plank of jarrah—hard, heavy Australian wood—that was exactly what I wanted for a piece of furniture I was planning. The plank was small, though, only 5 ft. long, 1¾ in. thick and less than 6 in. wide. The only way I could get much use out of it was to saw it into veneer. With some careful planning, I squeezed out of it all the veneers and edge-bandings I needed to make the sideboard in the photo above. The same plank, just about 4 bd. ft., wouldn't have been enough to make the top of the piece if I'd used it as solid.

I make my veneer on the bandsaw, as shown in the photo on the facing page, cutting sheets ³⁄₃₂ in. thick, which is thick enough to be worked much like solid wood with both hand and power tools. It's

also stiff enough to be edge-joined with wedge-clamp pressure. The finished surface is more forgiving and durable than thinner commercial veneer (generally, ¹⁄₂₈ in.). I also prefer shop-sawn veneer to the commercial variety because I can cut the solid-wood parts of a piece (legs, frame members, edge-bandings, pulls) from the same planks as the veneer. This means more control in matching grain and color patterns throughout the piece.

Veneer or solid wood?

There are several reasons I might decide to use veneer instead of solid wood in a piece of furniture. Clean lines and the lack of end grain give veneered work a refinement that fits some pieces better

Fig.1: Plank layout for veneered sideboard

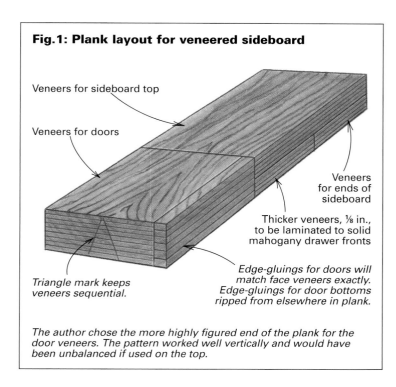

Veneers for sideboard top

Veneers for doors

Veneers for ends of sideboard

Thicker veneers, ⅛ in., to be laminated to solid mahogany drawer fronts

Triangle mark keeps veneers sequential.

Edge-gluings for doors will match face veneers exactly. Edge-gluings for door bottoms ripped from elsewhere in plank.

The author chose the more highly figured end of the plank for the door veneers. The pattern worked well vertically and would have been unbalanced if used on the top.

than others. If I were making a table or a case piece for a formal dining room, for instance, I'd consider using veneer; in a kitchen table, where veneer seems out of place, I'd probably use solid wood. Because wood movement is not a problem with veneered panels, they offer options not available with solid wood. The top of the sideboard, for example, has a pattern involving cross-grain pieces and inlay that would quickly self-destruct in solid wood.

Veneer can add strength, too. A veneered back panel, glued in, gives rigidity to a case. Veneered tops can be solidly attached and partitions and drawer runners can be glued into veneered carcases. All of this gives a strong and stable construction. For a detailed look at the ways I used veneer and solid wood, see the boxes on p. 24 and the drawing on p. 25.

One thing veneering won't do is save time. Doing quality veneer work always takes longer than working with solid wood, and I do it only when the possibilities it offers really fit the piece.

Laying out a plank

Before making any cuts, I take time to look at the milled plank or planks and decide how the grain patterns will work best with the various parts of the piece I'm planning, as shown in figure 1 above. I make sure there will be enough wood for all the veneers, plus pieces for edge-gluings and, in some cases, legs and stretchers. Both sides of every panel must be veneered to keep the stresses balanced, but for surfaces that won't show, I use veneer from less-desirable parts of the plank or from a different wood.

After deciding how to use the plank, I cut it into manageable pieces before sawing the veneer. Sawing veneer from large, heavy planks is difficult and best avoided. I look for places to crosscut long pieces and usually rip wide planks before sawing the veneer. Even if I had a bandsaw with 10 in. or 12 in. under the guides, I wouldn't attempt to saw veneer that wide. Better results will come by ripping the plank in half, sawing veneers from the narrower

Fig. 2: Finding a bandsaw blade's natural cutting angle

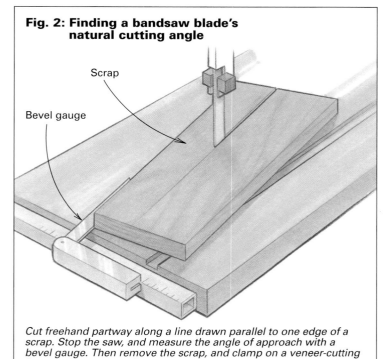

Scrap

Bevel gauge

Cut freehand partway along a line drawn parallel to one edge of a scrap. Stop the saw, and measure the angle of approach with a bevel gauge. Then remove the scrap, and clamp on a veneer-cutting fence at the same angle.

Fig. 3: Edging options for veneered panels

Veneer, ³⁄₃₂ in., can be applied as an edge-gluing after face veneers (above) or before (below), which leaves faces uninterrupted.

With larger edge-gluings, shapes can be worked on the edge with hand tools or a router.

Even cleanly cut plywood edges show a washboard effect. For a tight joint, take down the end-grain bumps with a slightly convex scraper or a narrow sanding block before gluing on the edging. Be sure to avoid shaving the face veneers.

Error-free edge-jointing—Prepare veneers for edge-gluing by jointing them in pairs on the shooting board. Lay one veneer face up and the other face down to compensate for any error in the angle of the plane blade.

pieces and then edge-joining the veneers to restore the full width.

Although I do a lot of careful planning, I try to remain flexible. A thick plank may have defects inside that make some of the veneer unusable. Or, if I'm lucky, there may be some beautiful color or pattern I hadn't anticipated. After looking at all the veneer, I may make changes in some of the dimensions or even major changes in the design to make the best use of the wood.

Sawing veneer

You don't need a large, expensive bandsaw to saw your own veneer, but you do need one that is well-tuned. Sharp blades are essential. Start with a new one, and change it when it starts to dull. The most obvious sign of dulling is increased resistance to feeding. But also, keep an eye on the quality of the cut. A dull blade leaves a more ragged surface and may give a bowed rather than a perfectly vertical cut. Half-inch skip tooth blades with 3 or 4 teeth per inch are good resaw blades. Larger blades often have too much set and produce more sawdust and fewer veneers.

The rip fence that comes with most bandsaws is inadequate for sawing veneer. A shopmade fence tall enough to support the full width of the wood and stopped just past the blade to let the sawn wood move will give much better results (see the photo on p. 21). Because it's held in place by clamps, you can angle it to follow the lead of the bandsaw blade. Bandsaw blades rarely want to cut at exactly 90° to the front of the table. To find the lead of the blade, draw a line parallel to one edge of a piece of scrap, and bandsaw freehand partway along the line. Then turn off the saw, and set a bevel gauge so that its handle is along the front edge of the bandsaw table and its blade is along the edge of the scrap, as shown in

figure 2 on p. 21. Use the bevel to set the veneer fence.

It is important to maintain constant pressure against the fence when cutting veneer. Use a smooth, steady feed rate from start to finish without stopping. I usually surface the plank with a light pass on the jointer between cuts. When the veneer is sawn, it should be stacked in the order it was cut and covered with a heavy piece of wood to keep it flat until you're ready to use it

If the sawing goes well and the veneers are consistent in thickness, it is possible to glue them to the core as they come from the saw. I usually take one or two light passes through the planer, though, to ensure uniform thickness.

I have a small Inca jointer with a thicknessing attachment that works well cleaning up the veneers. Its lack of a power feed is an advantage when planing veneer. Large power-feed planers, especially those with segmented feed rollers, tend to eat veneer. Clamping a piece of plywood across the infeed and outfeed tables, covering up the bed rollers, may solve this dietary problem. You can use the same arrangement if your planer won't adjust low enough to plane veneer.

Edge-joining veneers

The next step in preparing the veneer is edge-joining the pieces to get the widths I need. I lay out all the veneers, and then I make final decisions on how to use them, trying various patterns. I do this for all the surfaces at the same time so that I can see the effect of different arrangements. When I'm satisfied, I mark across the face of each group of veneers with a triangle to keep them in order. If there is any trimming to width or length to be done, I use the tablesaw just as I do with thicker stock.

Thick veneers edge-glue like solid wood. Lay the pieces to be joined between two fixed clamping boards. Hold the workpieces flat near the joint with one hand as you tighten a series of wedges with the other to apply pressure.

Fig. 4: Clamp-and-caul veneer press

Softwood cauls, crowned about ¹⁄₁₆ in. along the bottom edge, contact the middle first and distribute pressure across the glue-up.

Core stock

Mat board conforms to variations in the veneer.

Veneer

Layers of ¾-in. medium-density fiberboard spread the clamping pressure and ensure a flat panel.

Veneer is held in register during glue-up with brads or tape.

Shoot the edges—I take a pair of veneers to be joined and, using a shooting board, shoot the edges with a sharp jointer plane, as shown in the photo on the facing page. I do the shooting with one veneer face side up, the other face down. This compensates for a plane that may not be cutting at exactly 90° to the shooting board. Then I try the joint: It should be tight along its entire length with little pressure. Because veneers are somewhat flexible, it is possible to pull a badly fitting joint together, but don't be tempted. Take the time to shoot one or both edges again until the fit is right.

Wedge-glue the edge joints—The edge-joining goes quickly. With the veneers on a flat surface, I use pairs of wooden wedges to apply pressure, as shown in the photo above. Two strips of wood clamped to the benchtop are all you need for stops. They should be parallel, and about ½ in. farther apart than the width of the two veneers. I put a bead of glue on the edge of one veneer; then I put both veneers down between the wooden strips and push the joint together. A strip of newspaper keeps me from gluing to the benchtop. I use one hand to press down on the veneers at the joint while using the other to tighten the wedges. With all the wedges hand tight, I check the joint and then tap the wedges with a small hammer to set them. This technique makes it easy to keep the veneers flat during glue-up and also works well when gluing other thin stock, like drawer bottoms. Accurately jointed edges require minimal clamping pressure, which keeps the veneer from buckling.

Core materials

I generally glue sawn veneer to a core of Baltic-birch plywood. It is readily available in a variety of thicknesses and is strong. Lum-ber core plywood also works well but, unfortunately, can rarely be found in anything but ¾ in. thickness in this country. Medium-density fiberboard (MDF) and sheet goods of this type might be suitable, too, but I avoid them. I'm not convinced they're strong enough for some applications, and I don't like the smell and the dust they make in the shop. And MDF is terrible for planes and other hand tools. In some cases, when I need an unusual thickness, I'll make my own plywood core stock. I just stack an odd number of veneers with the grain in each sheet running at 90° to its neighbors and glue them together in my veneer press.

It's important that your core stock be flat. Buy it flat, and store it so it stays flat. You can stack it horizontally or vertically, as long as it's fully supported. Lean it against a wall, and it's sure to warp. Some warpage can be flattened in the veneering process, but it's better not to count on it. Perfectly flat core stock is vital for surfaces that will be unsupported, like cabinet doors or desk fall flaps.

Prepare for the press

With all the veneers edge-joined and the plywood cut to size, I get ready to glue up. If any of the plywood is going to get edge-gluings before veneering, I do that next. (For a range of options in edging veneered panels, see figure 3 on the facing page.)

I use a cabinet scraper to clean up the glue squeeze-out at joints in the veneer. Then I give both sides of the plywood and the bottom surface of the veneers a quick rub with 280-grit sandpaper: An oxidized surface is no good for gluing. Neither is a dusty one, so I clean off the sanded surfaces with the brush attachment on my shop vacuum and wipe them down with a clean cloth. Finally, it's a good idea to mark the veneers and core clearly, so a veneer

Flush-trimming edging is a two-plane procedure. One is set for a coarse cut; the other is set for a fine cut. On edge-gluings applied before face veneers, the outside corners must be crisp for a good joint.

doesn't get turned the wrong way during the glue-up.

I use yellow glue for most veneering. For something that will take a long time to clamp up (a large tabletop or a curved door), plastic resin glue will give a longer open time. I spread the glue with a scrap of veneer that has an edge notched on the bandsaw. (The kerfs are about ⅛ in. deep, and the teeth between them are the same width as the kerfs, ¹⁄₁₆ in. or so.) Working quickly, I spread the glue evenly on one side of the plywood and then place the veneer on the glued surface. I turn the whole thing over, glue the other side of the plywood and apply the veneer to that side. To keep the veneers from shifting in the press, I hammer a few small brads into what will become waste at each end. If there is no extra length that can be cut off after the glue-up, I use masking tape to hold everything in place. I start a piece of tape on the face of one veneer, pull it down tightly over the edge of the core and onto the other veneer. Three or four pieces along each side of the panel should keep things from shifting.

Into the veneer press

The basic clamp-and-caul veneer press shown in figure 4 on p. 23 is probably the simplest and least expensive setup for pressing veneers, but there are many possibilities. Veneer screws in frames are powerful, if bulky. A vacuum press, if you do enough veneering to justify the cost, is ideal. It equalizes the pressure perfectly over the entire surface of the veneer and can be used to do curved as well as flat surfaces. If you use a setup like mine, tighten the clamps in the center of the panel first, and move outward toward the edges. This avoids trapping glue in the center of the panel.

I usually leave a panel in the press for at least four hours. When it comes out of the press, the glue will have set, but the panel will still contain a lot of moisture from the glue. Never let a freshly veneered panel dry faster on one side than the other, or it will cup. When a panel comes out of the press, I stand it on end, so it is exposed to the air on both sides. Another alternative is to put it flat on the bench, cover it with a piece of plywood or MDF and weight it down. Once a panel dries completely (in one or two days), it will be stable.

When the panel is dry, I straighten and square one edge on the jointer. I trim the other three sides on the tablesaw to within ¹⁄₃₂ or so of final dimension and clean up the edges with a jointer plane. Then I'm ready to apply the edge-gluings or cut the joints. □

Paul Harrell is a furnituremaker in Pittsboro, N.C.

Creating a pattern with sawn veneer

I made the pattern on the top of my sideboard by joining the veneers before gluing them to the plywood core. I began by edge-gluing four narrow pieces of jarrah for the center section. I squared the ends of this section using a crosscut box on the tablesaw. Then I lightly shot the ends with a sharp jointer plane to eliminate irregularities in the sawn surface. Next I glued the end veneers of the mahogany frame to the center section. The joint is edge grain to end grain, so I used a gap-filling glue from Garrett Wade (161 Avenue of the Americas, New York, N.Y., 10013, 800-221-2942) that has a high solids content and fills the end grain nicely. I glued on these end pieces ¹⁄₃₂ in. over long and flushed them to the jarrah afterward. Then I glued on the front and back veneers of the mahogany frame. All these glue-ups were done with wedges (see the article on p. 20).

I glued the completed top pattern to the core in my press set up (see figure 4 on p. 23), simultaneously gluing a sheet of mahogany to the underside of the core. As with all veneer glue-ups, I cut the veneer so that its width and length were fractionally less than the core stock. When this came out of the press, I trimmed and planed the edges and applied ⅛-in. mahogany edge-gluings, mitered at the front corners and butted at the back. I cut the miters on the tablesaw and did final fitting with a 45° block on my shooting board. I trimmed the edgings flush to the veneer with a pair of handplanes (see the photo above). If there is any chance of tearout in the face veneer, I finish with a scraper. With the edge-gluings on, I routed a ⅛-in. by ⅛-in. rabbet around the top edge and glued a jarrah edge bead into it. I ripped the bead on the bandsaw and glued it in with the bandsawn edge outward. I use masking tape as a clamp, starting alternate pieces from below (inward pressure) and above (downward pressure). And I don't spare the tape. When I'm finished, there isn't any wood showing around the edge. —*P.H.*

Structural advantages of veneered panels

Veneered panels deliver a number of clear advantages over the traditional solid-wood frame and panel, which has to accommodate wood movement and relies solely on its frame for rigidity. The drawing on the facing page illustrates the advantages of veneered panels in a variety of applications.

End panels, 1 in. thick, create a large gluing surface, free from wood movement, for a rock-solid end assembly. The construction can eliminate the need for stretchers.

Back panel, ⅜ in., is glued into a rabbet, providing racking resistance. Bottom panels are also glued in place.

Partitions: Because the partitions won't move with the seasons, the drawer-runner frames can be let into them and glued along their full length.

Doors: The stability of the plywood core is particularly welcome in an unfixed member like a door. Besides keeping the doors flat, the lack of seasonal movement permits fitting to much closer tolerances in the door opening.

Top: Because it won't move, the top can be joined solidly to the ends, stretchers and partitions, increasing resistance to sagging. The stability also permits cross-grain patterning. —*P.H.*

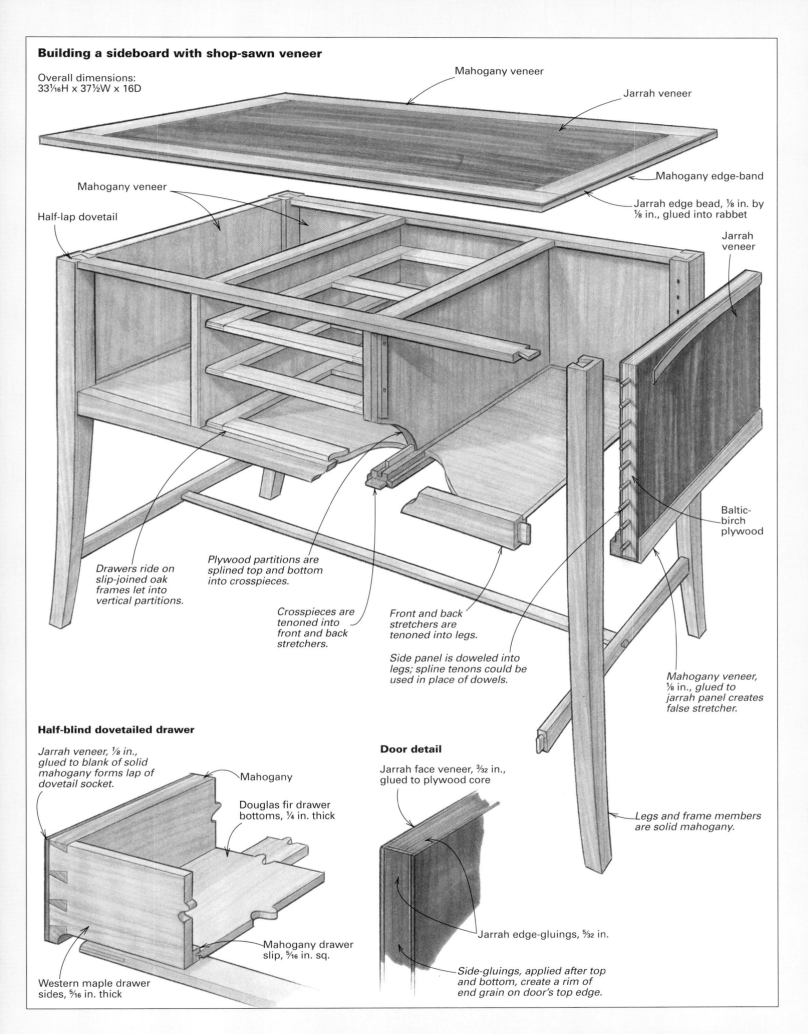

Building a sideboard with shop-sawn veneer

Overall dimensions:
33 1/16H x 37 1/2W x 16D

Mahogany veneer

Jarrah veneer

Mahogany edge-band

Jarrah edge bead, 1/8 in. by 1/8 in., glued into rabbet

Mahogany veneer

Half-lap dovetail

Jarrah veneer

Baltic-birch plywood

Drawers ride on slip-joined oak frames let into vertical partitions.

Plywood partitions are splined top and bottom into crosspieces.

Crosspieces are tenoned into front and back stretchers.

Front and back stretchers are tenoned into legs.

Side panel is doweled into legs; spline tenons could be used in place of dowels.

Mahogany veneer, 1/8 in., glued to jarrah panel creates false stretcher.

Legs and frame members are solid mahogany.

Half-blind dovetailed drawer

Jarrah veneer, 1/8 in., glued to blank of solid mahogany forms lap of dovetail socket.

Mahogany

Douglas fir drawer bottoms, 1/4 in. thick

Mahogany drawer slip, 5/16 in. sq.

Western maple drawer sides, 5/16 in. thick

Door detail

Jarrah face veneer, 3/32 in., glued to plywood core

Jarrah edge-gluings, 5/32 in.

Side-gluings, applied after top and bottom, create a rim of end grain on door's top edge.

Easy Veneering with a Household Iron

Dried glue, heat and pressure bond a lovely wood skin onto any project

by Mario Rodriguez

Ironing on veneer is simple and quick even on curves like this apron. First apply yellow glue to both the substrate and the veneer; let them dry. Then place the two together, and reactivate the glue with an ordinary iron.

Photos: Alec Waters

Being able to veneer can dramatically extend the scope of projects available to a woodworker. You can take veneer, a beautiful but unstable material, and apply it to a solid, flat substrate. You can also repeat or book-match patterns for a spectacular effect. But what's the best way to glue down the veneer and keep it down?

Mentioning traditional techniques of hot hide glue and a veneer hammer produces accelerated pulses and sweaty palms for most woodworkers. In my veneering workshops when students get over their initial fear of gluing veneer, they are okay.

But when I visited former apprentice Ken Vigiletti, he turned me on to another way of applying veneer using waterproof yellow glue and a household electric iron (see the photo on the facing page). At first, I was skeptical. But after seeing a demonstration, I was anxious to get back to my shop to give the technique a try. And the project I had in mind—a small half-round hall table that I wanted to cover with sycamore veneer—was perfect because veneer would enhance the table's form (see the photo at right).

Vigiletti's demonstration was not the first time I'd seen veneer adhered with an iron. The technique also appeared in *FWW* #87, p. 66 (this book, p. 68). But in that article, the author applied white glue to the substrate and then immediately ironed on the veneer. With that method, the veneer can slide on the wet glue, causing misalignment and gaps at the seams. By contrast, when you heat the dry glue through the veneer, it adheres in place right away. And water is less likely to evaporate out of the glue and through the veneer, causing bubbles.

About the adhesive
The main appeal of veneering with yellow glue is that many of us use it daily. With yellow glue, you don't have to worry about water-to-glue ratios, soaking time, temperature, hammering pressure or the mess associated with hide glue. And by using an ordinary iron, there's no need for a vacuum bag, an expensive press or any complicated clamping cauls. But because I wasn't keen about the idea of having to redo the veneer if the bond failed, I was still hesitant about heating waterproof glue with an iron. So I asked one of *Fine Woodworking*'s regular contributors, Chris Minick, about the process. Minick, a research chemist, heartily endorsed the technique (see the box on p. 28).

Even before talking to Minick, I was attracted to the prospect of ironing veneer over waterproof glue for a couple of reasons. In situations where the wood will be exposed to moisture, such as in a sink cabinet or in a vanity for a bathroom, the veneer isn't likely to come loose. Also, once this type of glue is cured, it isn't sensitive to common finishing solvents, so finishing shouldn't affect the veneer bond.

Another advantage of this method is that you can glue down burl or crotch veneer without getting glue stains, which can cause finish delamination and uneven staining. When you glue down these veneers using a press, the glue bleeds through. This is because of the capillary action caused by the high percentage of end grain. Unless you use hide glue, the glue stains are nearly impossible to remove. However, by allowing the yellow glue to set up beforehand, you create a barrier near the surface that minimizes the bleed-through.

While I was talking to Minick, I learned of another technique that prevents the glue from bleeding through onto the face of the veneer. First seal the back side with shellac (use a 3-lb. cut). Once the shellac is dry, apply the glue and wait for it to dry. Then you can iron the veneer. Minick, who used the method on some quilted mahogany veneer, said that the shellac undercoat works well because shellac is thermoplastic, just like the glue and just like the burn-in repair sticks that furniture repairers and restorers use. And, if you get a dab of shellac on the veneer face, no big deal. Shellac is a great sealer; it's compatible with virtually any finish.

Cutting and taping the veneer
On the table project, I started by veneering the tapered legs (the legs made good practice before I did the top) and ended with the more difficult curved apron. I cut veneer for the legs using a sharp chip-carving knife. When veneering the top, I used narrow strips of veneer tape along the seam, and I reinforced the joint with shorter straps of tape running perpendicularly.

Veneer can emphasize a table's form.
To bring out this table's traditional shapes, like tapered Federal-style legs, the author veneered it with sycamore. The table is suitable for an entrance hall or this formal dining room at the historic Peach Grove Inn in Warwick, N.Y.

Stabilizing and gluing veneer—With a scrapwood backup, Rodriguez rolls glue onto the back of the veneer. By spraying water on the face of the veneer, he keeps the piece from curling. He has already smoothed the front of the apron and coated its surface with glue.

Scraping the veneer leaves a clean, smooth surface. Once the glue is cured and the veneer is set, the author uses a scraper to remove skid and scorch marks left by the iron. He keeps the scraper even and the strokes light to prevent the burr from digging into the surface.

Before gluing, I also taped all the cracks, which is especially important if you're using curly veneer. To see if there are any splits, hold the veneer up to a light. If there are any cracks of light, even slightly suspect areas, tape them.

Some veneers, like burls and crotches, require a substrate veneer laid 90° under the face veneer. This underlayment absorbs the movement of the face veneer and prevents tiny surface checks. Because of the relatively straight grain and the ⅛ in. thickness of the sycamore veneer (most veneer is ¹⁄₆₄ in. thick), I omitted this step on my table.

Applying the glue

To apply the Titebond II glue, I used a small paint roller with a short nap. I heavily coated both the substrate and the back of the veneer. Before setting the veneer to dry, I sprayed the face side with a little water to minimize any curl (see the top photo). One thing to remember when you're working with veneer: What you do to one side, do to the other. In this case, the water mimics the glue.

Ironing the veneer

After setting down the veneer to dry for about 30 minutes, I placed the veneer with some overhang all around. Then, using a steam iron on the cotton setting, I pressed the veneer firmly and worked from the center out. I kept the pressure steady and the iron moving slowly. Looking for any gaps or open seams, I went over the veneer several times, allowing the iron to linger over any trouble spots. If you leave too much overhang on the veneer, the edges could curl away from the substrate, preventing a clean, tight job. To remedy this, limit overhang to ⅛ in., and apply steam from the iron. The steam causes the veneer to expand on the face side, which allows it to lie flat again.

The iron left some light skid and scorch marks, but these were easily scraped off

later after the glue cured (see the bottom photo). On larger areas, I work from the center out toward the edges to avoid creating bubbles or creases. But I've learned that every veneer behaves differently—even within the same species. So on certain jobs, you may want to iron the edges first. Experiment on scrap to see.

The heat from the iron should drive out excess moisture from the glue, which might otherwise bubble up under the veneer. Steam also works to temporarily release the veneer when you want to reposition it or when you need to iron out blisters and bubbles.

On my table project, the veneer was large enough to cover the apron in one piece, but often I have to join narrow pieces to span a larger surface. You can shoot and tape the seams prior to gluing, and then treat the assembly as one piece. Or you

How thermoplastic adhesives work

by Chris Minick

Ironing on veneer is a sound idea. It'll work with yellow glue, white glue and waterproof yellow glue (such as Titebond II) because all are types of polyvinyl acetate (PVA), which are thermoplastic adhesives. This means the solid resin (dry glue) becomes flowable (plastic) at a certain temperature. The range can be from under 200° to over 400°F. To visualize this phenomenon, picture your sandpaper gumming up when you sand hardened glue. The heat produced by friction causes the glue to melt. This same thermoplastic attribute will allow you to veneer with an iron.

A household electric iron (not a travel iron) will produce enough heat to melt most PVA glues. The glue will become workable and sticky for a period of time. But here's where there are differ-

Video: Ironing on veneer

VIDEO TAKES

If you like the look of veneer, but you don't like the mess of hot-hide glue or the fuss of vacuum bags and clamping cauls, Mario Rodriguez will show you a slick way to glue down ve-can lay the veneer one piece at a time, and cut your seams in place. You do this by overlapping the second piece onto the first and cutting through both of them. After passing your saw or knife over the seam several times, lift the top waste piece away from the seam. Then gently lift the edge of the top sheet, and remove the waste strip from the bottom piece of veneer. If you can't lift the veneer, use a bit of steam from the iron to loosen up things. When both waste strips are removed, press the seam firmly. After ironing, apply veneer tape lengthwise down the seam, and place tape straps across the seam (which prevents the seam from creeping open). Leave the tape in place for 24 to 48 hours.

Trimming the veneer

To trim the veneer for the hall table, I used a sequence of hand tools. First I cut the ve-

ences: Regular white glue can be reactivated indefinitely at a temperature of only around 180°F (below the "delicate" setting). Yellow (aliphatic resin) glue must be heated to about 250°F (between "delicate" and "wool"), and you might have a window of a week or more to do this. Waterproof glue requires a temperature of 350°F or more in the "cotton" to "linen" range. And because it's a cross-linking PVA, you're better off getting it ironed down within 72 hours. To find out exactly how long you have to reactivate your adhesive, call the manufacturer.

If you're unsure about your glue and how hot to set the iron, take some scrap veneer, and start ironing at a low temperature. Then use more and more heat until the glue is workable and you can adhere the veneer. Once you move the iron away, the glue will cool fairly quickly, and your veneer will be set in place. This minimal-heat approach may prevent you from overheating a piece of delicate veneer. □

Chris Minick is a product-development chemist in Stillwater, Minn.

neer using a household iron. He also goes into detail about trimming veneer and getting clean joints. And he shows how to handle difficult veneers like curly and crotch. Send for "Ironvid," a $10, 28-minute video cassette (VHS) companion to this article. Order #011039, The Taunton Press, P.O. Box 5506, Newtown, Conn. 06470; (203) 426-8171.—*Alec Waters, associate editor*

neer with a veneer saw, as shown in the top photo. I prefer a French veneer saw (which is available from the Garrett Wade Co. Inc., 161 Avenue of the Americas, New York, N.Y. 10013-1299; 800-221-2942) because its teeth point toward the center of the blade arc from both ends, which lets me score the veneer before beginning the cut. And because the handle is directly alongside the blade, a French veneer saw gives me better control than the more common offset-handle veneer saws.

Next, paying close attention to the direction of the veneer's grain, I use a block plane to trim the veneer almost flush with the adjacent surface. For this job, I use a Lie Nielsen block plane. And rather than risk tearing the veneer or digging into the wood, I leave the veneer edge proud. After planing, I use a 10-in.-long second-cut file to level the veneer to the substrate. I work from the edge into the veneer so that I don't chip it, and I lift the file on each return stroke.

Then I use a Sandvik scraper to smooth out the file marks, as shown in the center photo, while again noting the direction of the grain. The scraper leaves a clean surface that will ensure tight, almost invisible, seams. By keeping about three-fourths of the scraper on the work, I prevent the scraper's burr from rolling over the edge.

After gluing veneer to the adjoining surface and allowing it to dry, I repeat the above steps to trim the veneer where it meets at the corner. Finally, I slightly bevel the edge of the veneer at the joint using a smooth file (see the bottom photo). □

Mario Rodriguez teaches woodworking at the Fashion Institute of Technology in New York City, and offers traditional veneering clinics in Warwick, N.Y. He is a contributing editor to Fine Woodworking.

TRIMMING VENEER

Saw off the veneer leaving a little overhang to protect the edges. The author drags his veneer saw along the tabletop (top) leaving about 1/32 in. excess.

File and then scrape the surface flush, so the corner will be tight (center). After Rodriguez files the veneer edges level with the leg, he scrapes them smooth.

Chamfer adds a finishing touch—Using a smooth file (above), the author bevels the veneer edges, which eases and protects the table's corners and helps to disguise the seams.

Veneering over a Solid-Wood Substrate

Thirty-year old rosewood gives life to a shapely coffee table

by Tage Frid

I've been experimenting with veneering over solid woods for a while and have discovered some interesting design possibilities. One of them, which I've used on the table shown below, involves removing wood in such a way that I expose a graduated portion of the substrate along its edge. By first beveling the veneered tabletop and then bandsawing gentle curves along both sides and ends, the exposed maple seems thinner in the center and wider at the ends. The effect can be very dramatic or much more restrained. For this table, I wanted to maximize the contrast with the veneer—some prize rosewood I've been saving for 30 years—so I chose maple for the substrate. Whether you're looking for a subtle distinction or a loud contrast, the veneer adds an element to the design that would be impossible without it.

Some people think real woodworkers don't use veneers. This is small-minded thinking. Veneering has been around almost since man first started cutting trees. Indeed, some of the finest furniture ever made—fabulous 18th- and 19th-century pieces from France and England—used veneers extensively and over solid wood. Many of those pieces have stood the test of time.

When veneering over solid wood, orient the veneer in the same direction as the substrate. I used a vacuum veneer press, but clamps and cauls (wooden blocks to spread the clamping pressure) can also be used. Although I normally use regular yellow glue for veneering, I used plastic-resin glue for this table because it works better with oily woods like rosewood. In either case, it's essential that you spread the glue evenly and not too thickly. I use a paint roller with a rough, woven (washable) pad, which is designed for spreading contact cement. It's important to veneer both the top and bottom of the tabletop so that the wood can exchange moisture with the air evenly on both sides. I glued mahogany veneer on the bottom of this table.

I designed the legs of the table to complement the top. Because they're curved, I made sure the grain runs full length, so there are no short-grain sections that could be vulnerable. After shaping, mortising and veneering the legs, I spokeshaved the corners to expose a little bit of the maple.

The table's finish is Watco Danish Oil Finish—the simplest to apply and the easiest to repair. That's important, especially if you put your feet up on the coffee table as much as I do. □

Tage Frid is a contributing editor to Fine Woodworking.

Graceful curves and beautiful veneer *combine to give Tage Frid's most recent coffee-table design a classic, timeless look. The table, on display last fall at the Newport Art Museum, was one of several pieces by Frid in the Nine Rhode Island Masters of Modern Furniture show.*

Fig. 1: Rosewood-veneered coffee table

The most elegant designs are often the simplest. Tage Frid's most recent table design relies on fair curves, appropriate proportions and contrasting wood colors for its beauty.

Bottom view

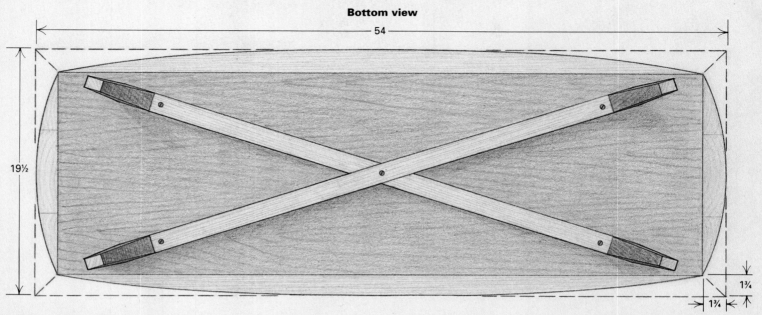

Stretchers are screwed to tabletop at center and just inside of each leg. Half-lap joint where stretchers overlap allows them to move with the tabletop, preventing any wood movement problems.

To mark the tabletop's curves for cutting, Frid tacked small brads 1¾ in. in from each corner, sprung a batten (centered on the middle of the table's edges) and penciled a line.

Side view

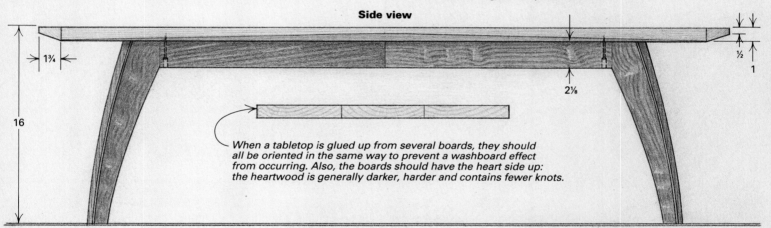

When a tabletop is glued up from several boards, they should all be oriented in the same way to prevent a washboard effect from occurring. Also, the boards should have the heart side up: the heartwood is generally darker, harder and contains fewer knots.

Fig. 2: Leg layout and clamping block

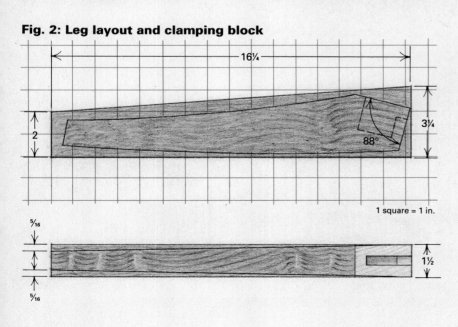

1 square = 1 in.

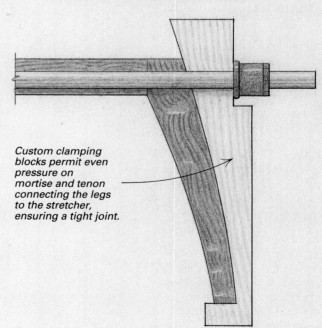

Custom clamping blocks permit even pressure on mortise and tenon connecting the legs to the stretcher, ensuring a tight joint.

1) Truing the edges of the veneers

2) Frid pins the veneers

3) Gummed package tape holds the veneers in place

4) Eliminating air pockets

5) Frid scrapes the package tape from the veneer

Veneer the tabletop, then shape its edges

1) Truing the edges of the veneers takes only a few seconds on the jointer. Frid aligns the veneers so that they're just barely protruding from a wooden sandwich, clamps the veneers between the two boards and then runs the clamped assembly over the jointer knives. Alternately, Frid could have used a hand plane, but the jointer is convenient and works as well or better.

2) Frid pins the veneers temporarily into place with small brads after carefully aligning the trued, book-matched sheets of veneer.

3) Gummed package tape holds the veneers in place while they're being transferred onto the substrate and into the vacuum bag. Frid doesn't use masking tape because its adhesive could tear the veneer's fibers or leave a residue that would interfere with finishing the table. Once he's taped the veneers together, Frid removes the brads he used to pin the veneers.

4) Eliminating air pockets that would interfere with even pressure on the tabletop, Frid presses the bag in at the corners. A sheet of plywood goes over the top of the

From *Fine Woodworking* (January 1993) 98:40-43

7) *Bandsawing to a line drawn along a sprung batten*

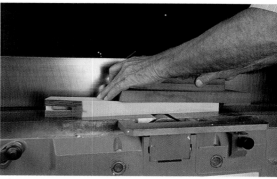

8) *Frid tapers both sides of each leg*

9) *Frid cleans up the curves*

piece being veneered, and extends just beyond its edges, to prevent the slightly oversized veneer from shearing on the edge of the substrate.

5) Frid scrapes the package tape from the veneer with a cabinet scraper after removing the veneered tabletop from the vacuum press.

6) Frid bevels the edge of the tabletop (see the top photo on p. 30) after he's ripped it to width and crosscut it to length. An auxiliary plywood fence, a firmly clamped, solid featherboard and the assistance of his apprentice (and grandson), Ben Randall, keep Frid safe and the bevel true.

7) Bandsawing to a line drawn along a sprung batten, Frid exposes a graduated section of the solid maple substrate from the center of each side to the ends; a few passes with a compass plane take care of any rough edges. The result is an interesting treatment achieved with simple means.

8) Frid tapers both sides of each leg by 5⁄16 in. from top to bottom, cutting away the bulk of the taper on the bandsaw and then jointing to the line. He uses a shopmade push block to keep his hands safely away from the jointer knives.

9) Frid cleans up the curves with a spokeshave after veneering the jointed sides of the legs and marking and bandsawing the curves for the legs. A smooth surface is essential because these two faces are also veneered.

Veneering a Tabletop

Iron down veneer one piece at a time for tight seams and a reliable bond

by Michael Burton

Sitting in a dimly lit room, the old pool table looked more or less sound. Some of the veneer had started to peel, and the owner was anxious to know whether the table could be repaired. "Of course it can," I told him.

Later, when I took the table and my bravado into the shop, it was a different story. Lots of veneer had to be replaced. I started to worry about the hot hide glue I'd always used for veneering. The glue holds down veneer just fine, but wood that isn't veneered on both sides can warp. I didn't see a way to get the table apart to get at both sides of all the pieces, at least not easily. I was stuck.

Before long, I was experimenting with aliphatic resin glue. I learned that once dried, this glue can be reactivated with a house-hold iron to form a very good bond. Best of all, veneer applied this way to only one side of the workpiece doesn't cause any distortion. The pool table was salvaged. Ever since, I've been using this iron-on technique on everything from repairs to new tabletops as large as 7 ft. dia.

The technique is simple. Glue is applied to both the veneer and the ground (the material the veneer is glued to). After the glue has dried, the two materials are ironed together. The heat from the iron melts the glue and bonds the two surfaces (for more on using this technique to veneer small surfaces, see pp. 26-29).

You don't need any special or expensive equipment like bulky veneer presses or vacuum bags (mine is now gathering dust in a

Two coats of glue on both surfaces. *The author uses a brush to spread thinned glue on the top of this game table.*

corner of the shop). Nor is it necessary to join several pieces of veneer together with veneer tape before covering a large surface; the seams are made as the sheets are applied. This technique works with wrinkled veneers, even burls and crotches, and it may save you the trouble of flattening such rare and beautiful woods before application.

Like any other technique, though, ironing down veneer has its quirks. If you've tried this approach, you know that heat produced by an iron can shrink the veneer, opening up seams and causing some checking if you're not careful. When used with a little fore-thought, however, these problems are minimal at worst. The keys to success are pre-shrinking the veneer before ironing it down, applying the glue in several thinned coats and cutting the seams as you go. This is the same approach I used to veneer a small game table that my shop was recently commissioned to make (see the photo on the facing page). The iron-on method worked perfectly, and I'll show you how I did it.

Test veneer for shrinkage, and repair any holes

Before thinking about glue, the veneer should be checked for heat tolerance. Some species can shrink dramatically under the heat that will be required to bond them with dry glue. To check, mea-sure a piece of veneer across the grain, and then heat the wood with your iron at the three-quarter setting (see the photo at right). After the veneer has cooled for a few minutes, measure again. If the shrinkage is significant, it's a good idea to pre-shrink all of the veneer you plan to use by thoroughly heating it with the iron. Even though the glue will swell the veneer when it's applied, pre-shrinking the material now reduces the chance of checks and open seams later.

If there are any defects in the veneer, such as holes or checks, now's the time to tape them on the face side. A number of wood-working suppliers sell veneer tape. It's just a strip of paper with adhesive on one side that you wet and stick down. When you're all done, you can scrape the tape off. It's not a good idea to use masking tape; heat from the iron will turn it into a gummy mess, and masking tape stretches.

The veneer tape will hold the veneer together and prevent the glue from reaching the face. If you're working with paper-backed veneer, which has a layer of paper bonded to the back side of the veneer, scuff the paper with 80-grit sandpaper before applying the glue. If you don't do this, the glaze on the paper can cause prob-lems in getting an even glue coat.

Because I cut the seams as I go along, there's no need to fit the veneer precisely to the ground at this point. I lay out where the seams will be on the ground with a sharp pencil and make sure that the pieces of veneer will cover the area with a little bit to spare. With these steps out of the way, I can apply glue to both the veneer and the ground.

Spread the glue in several coats

Glue thinned about 10% with water spreads easier and covers bet-ter than one coat straight from the bottle. I use either Titebond or Elmer's yellow glue, thinning it until it's the consistency of heavy cream. Complete coverage is important, and a brush works much better than a roller (see the photo at right). A roller can leave air bubbles and an undesirable texture and is totally ineffective on wrinkled veneer.

Spreading glue on the ground is very straightforward—just brush on a good, even coat (see the photo on the facing page). Before spreading glue on the veneer, it's a good idea to mist some water from a spray bottle on the face side. This will help eliminate curl-ing caused by the moisture of the glue on the back. After the glue

Getting the shrink out. Because some veneers shrink dramati-cally during the bonding process, the author starts by pre-shrink-ing all the veneer with the iron at a three-quarter setting.

Thin the glue, and paint it on. Aliphatic resin glue thinned about 10% with water spreads easily with a brush, eliminating the bubbles that can occur with a roller.

Photos except where noted: Scott Gibson

BONDING ONE PIECE AT A TIME

Bond first, trim later. *With layout lines drawn on the tabletop, the author bonds the first piece of padauk veneer in the pattern. He keeps the iron away from edges that need trimming.*

A sharp linoleum knife works best. *With a straightedge and a linoleum knife, the author trims the edge of the first piece of veneer. Knife marks are extended beyond the edge as a reference for trimming the next piece of veneer accurately.*

has been spread on the back side of the veneer, place the veneer on sticks so that air circulates around both sides.

If possible, stay with the veneer as the glue dries. If puddles form, spread them out with a putty knife or a scrap of plastic laminate. Make sure that edges that will be part of a seam are well-covered with glue. After the first coat of glue has dried (*dry* means that all of the creamy white color has been replaced with a transparent light yellow), feel the surface. If it has become rough, sand lightly with 80-grit paper. Then put a second coat of glue on both the veneer and the ground.

Some species of veneer and some ground materials, such as the raw edge of medium-density fiberboard (MDF), may require a third or even a fourth coat. The object is to have a smooth, glossy, transparent film of glue that looks a little like a thick coat of varnish. Veneer will have a leather-like feel when it's properly coated with glue.

Once you have enough glue on both surfaces and it has dried, pass a sanding block with 80-grit paper lightly over the ground and, if possible, the veneer. This will knock the top off any dust, coagulated glue or whatever may have settled on the glue as it was drying. Anything that the sandpaper won't smooth out should be cut off with a sharp knife or a chisel.

It's just like ironing your shirt

Now it's time to iron down the first piece of veneer. Position a rough-cut piece of veneer so that it overlaps any seams by ¼ in. or so (how much overlap you can afford will depend on the veneer and your pattern, but don't leave any less than ⅛ in.). Heat, residual moisture and wrinkles can often distort the veneer as it's bonded. This is the reason I prefer trimming after the bonding process. With the iron turned up about halfway, use the tip to tack the veneer in place. Then with slow, circular motions, proceed to bond this first piece of veneer, staying ¼ in. or so away from areas that will be trimmed later (see the top photo).

How hard do you press the iron? Don't break the handle! But remember that the heated glue is plastic, not fluid, so the more pressure the better. There is no law against using two hands. You will often hear clicking sounds as you iron. These are small spots pulling loose. You should iron until the clicking stops. Keep the iron moving—don't linger in any spot. Overheating the glue will destroy its bonding characteristics.

Should you encounter a real stubborn wrinkle, moisten the area with a damp cloth, and iron it immediately. Don't give the area a chance to swell. The added moisture and heat will cause the area to compress, and the steam will penetrate the veneer to aid the glue bond. I've heard the suggestion that a steam iron be used for bonding. This works for single pieces and large sections of paper-backed veneer, but in a design with a lot of seams, the added moisture often can cause dimensional changes in the veneer that are completely intolerable. Keep your work as dry as possible.

Trim the first seam, and then test the bond

With the first piece bonded, I trim the seams with a sharp linoleum knife, my tool of choice. I just think of it as a veneer saw with one tooth. And like a saw, it works best when you make the cut in a number of passes.

When cutting the seam, I let the knife overcut the veneer into the border areas (see the photo at left). These marks will be used for lining up the straightedge for trimming the next piece. Should you encounter areas of waste that have been accidentally bonded, cut them loose with a sharp chisel (a dogleg is excellent for the job). If

From *Fine Woodworking* (September 1995) 114:56-59

the glue has been removed from the ground, re-spread those spots.

After trimming, you may wish to check the bond. I always do. With your fingernail or a stiff brush, go over the surface and listen for a hollow sound indicating that the veneer isn't bonded. Then I moisten the veneer with a damp cloth. Loose spots will manifest themselves as bubbles. If you are working in a quiet area, the veneer often will talk to you. A clicking sound will be heard as the bubbles pull themselves loose. If any loose spots are detected, use the tip of the iron and a little extra pressure to bond them, and then pass the iron over the entire piece to dry it.

Cutting and fitting the next piece

That first piece is now well-bonded. In fact, if you tried to pry it up, the veneer would take chunks of the MDF with it. The next step is to rough-cut the second piece and position it for bonding. If you are working with flat veneer that doesn't seem to wrinkle much under heat, you may wish to precut the second piece and shoot the edge with a sanding block. If this is the case, let the piece overlap the first by about .01 in. (about the thickness of a match-book cover). Then bond the second piece of veneer, staying about 1½ in. back from the seam.

The secret to a tight seam is that little extra you've allowed. Take that .01 in. of overlap, and buckle the veneer slightly so that the seam edges are butted together. A piece of ³⁄₁₆-in. steel or brass rod pushed beneath the second piece of veneer near the edge is a great help (see the center photo). If the trimmed seam is a little ragged, carefully pass a sandpaper block over it. And if you are the type who wears a belt and suspenders simultaneously, you also may wish to brush a light coat of fresh glue on the edge of the veneer. I have often done this where I feared the veneer shrinking and the seam opening up.

After the pieces are butted together, withdraw the rod, and iron down the buckled seam (see the bottom photo). Position the iron so it spans the whole seam. The veneer often splits when the tip of the iron rides the center of the buckled area, so make sure the entire area is covered with the sole of the iron. A joint made in this manner places a great amount of pressure at the seam and is highly unlikely to open up.

If your veneer is wrinkled, the procedure is slightly different but gets you the same result. Let the second piece overlap the first by at least ¼ in.; then iron it down except for the 1½ in. next to the seam. After the veneer is down, trim the edge to be seamed with the first piece.

Make the cut so the second piece overlaps the first by about .01 in. (see the top photo). Cut through the top piece only. I use a scrap of plastic laminate to protect the bottom piece of veneer. This is not a double-cut. Do I have to tell you to work carefully? You have only one chance.

Test the surface with a damp cloth

I use this one-piece-at-a-time approach until I've covered the top with veneer. I make sure the veneer is well-bonded by dampening the surface with water and looking for bubbles. Bubbles detected now are easy to fix with an iron. If you find one later, don't panic. A product called Brasive (Mohawk Finishing Products Co., 4715 State Highway 30, Amsterdam, NY 12010-7417; 518-843-1380) introduced through a pin hole in the bubble will reactivate the glue and bond the veneer without reheating. □

Michael Burton and his three sons make furniture in a variety of styles at Burton's Furniture Studios in Ogden, Utah.

MAKING A TIGHT SEAM

For wrinkled veneer, cut the seam in place. *Heat can distort the edges of some veneers, so the author may choose to cut a clean edge once the second piece of veneer is mostly bonded.*

Secret for a tight seam. *For a seam that won't pull open from the heat of the iron, the author cuts the second piece of veneer .010 in. wide. Then he buckles it over a piece of ³⁄₁₆-in. rod so that the edges meet.*

Iron down the hump. *Working from one end and withdrawing the rod as he goes, the author presses down the seam. It will stay tight.*

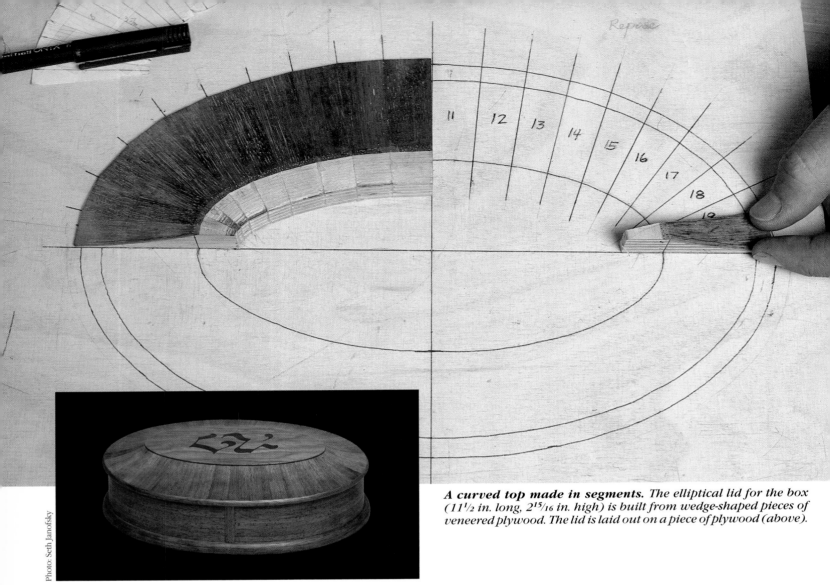

Photo: Seth Janofsky

A curved top made in segments. *The elliptical lid for the box (11½ in. long, 2¹⁵/₁₆ in. high) is built from wedge-shaped pieces of veneered plywood. The lid is laid out on a piece of plywood (above).*

Veneering a Compound Curve

Wedge-shaped pieces form a delicate, elliptical box lid

by John Gallagher

The unexpected is one thing I can count on whenever I make objects intended to please the hand and eye. I enjoy the unpredictability. It seems like an essential ingredient in creative work, and it played a part in the creation of the box in the photo at left. Once I was content with the design, I began to think about the pragmatic problem-solving that goes along with construction. The box held promise as an elegant and challenging project, with an element of uncertainty in exactly how it might be built.

The centerpiece of this box in kwila wood is its elliptical lid. I considered carving the lid from solid wood. But something of the original spirit of the piece would have been lost. My design sketch showed a radiating grain pattern in the top, nothing like the effect I would have achieved from a solid piece of wood. That pushed me toward a veneered lid, which would allow the grain to flow outward from the top toward the edge. A veneered top would be less susceptible to seasonal change, which seemed like an advantage, and veneering a compound curved surface intrigued me.

The curved sides of the box were fairly simple—thin laminations glued up around a form. But how do I veneer the lid, a surface that curves in not one but two planes? I doubted the joints would hold if I edge-joined pieces of veneer with a handplane and pressed them to fit a curved substrate. The answer that held the most promise was building the curved lid from a number of small wedge-shaped pieces. If the pieces, viewed in section, had a curved, tapered shape, they would produce a form of curved facets something like a Victrola speaker, which is close to a compound curve. By cutting a sweeping cove in one face of a piece of narrow stock and gluing the veneer to it, I'd have the rough stock

Photos except where noted: Jonathan Binzen

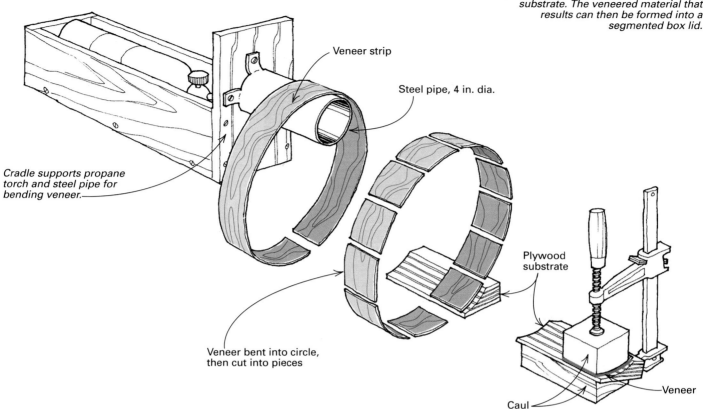

A section of metal pipe heated by a propane torch coaxes veneer strips into curved shapes. Cut into smaller pieces, the veneer is glued to a plywood substrate. The veneered material that results can then be formed into a segmented box lid.

Veneer strip

Steel pipe, 4 in. dia.

Cradle supports propane torch and steel pipe for bending veneer.

Plywood substrate

Veneer bent into circle, then cut into pieces

Veneer

Caul

for the lid pieces. Then it was a matter of cutting the stock into pie-shaped pieces and gluing them into an elliptical shape.

Cutting a cove in the substrate

To make the substrate, I started with ⅝-in. Baltic-birch plywood about 7 in. wide. I ripped it to the correct width, 2⅝ in., after cutting the cove. Plywood is more stable than solid wood, and the high-quality Baltic ply is of uniform thickness and without voids.

Cutting coves on the tablesaw usually involves running the stock flat on the table over the blade (for more on this technique, see *FWW* #102, pp. 82-85). But to approximate the cove I wanted, I had to mill the material running on edge, with the top slightly shimmed away from the top of the fence (see the photo at right). The advantage was that the material was registered on the side opposite the one being cut, providing an unchanging reference point. Any variations in the thickness of the ply didn't show up in the thin edge of the cove. The usual method would be to run the stock flat over the sawblade, but removing most of the material on one side would have left little wood for support.

I set a fence at 90° to the blade on the tablesaw and made a series of light passes to produce a symmetrical cove with a 5-in. radius. To keep as much of the blade out of the way while I cut the cove, I put a sawkerf in a piece of 2x4 and clamped that to the saw table over the blade.

A hot pipe to bend the veneer

To form the curved pieces of veneer for the lid, I borrowed an idea from luthiers. I made a hot pipe bending jig from a piece of 4-in.

This cove needed a long, sweeping profile. *The plywood used to make the lid pieces required a graceful cove on one face. To get it, the author ran the material across the tablesaw blade on edge and tilted away from the fence. An extra piece of 2x4 covers most of the blade during the cut.*

Drawings: author (rendered by Jim Richey)

Small cutoff jig makes lid pieces. *After laying out the segments, the author cut them to size on a small jig with an adjustable fence that fits on a tablesaw.*

Fig. 2: Making lid pieces

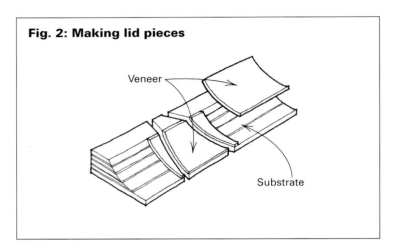

Veneer

Substrate

Fine adjustment for fit. *A plane and a shooting board helped the author trim pieces, so they conformed exactly to the elliptical plan he worked from.*

steel pipe (see figure 1 on p. 39). After setting up the pipe on a cradle, I trained a ½-in.-long blue flame from a propane torch on the inside top of the pipe until water sprayed on the pipe quickly boiled off. If water just sits there and steams, the pipe is too cool. If water bounces off the pipe, it's too hot.

I bandsaw my own veneer, so I can control wood tone and grain. I sawed everything I needed for the box from the same stock. For the lid pieces, the veneer strips were ³⁄₃₂ in. thick, 2 in. wide and 18 in. long, and I bent them over the pipe into circles. I checked the curve against a cardboard template to make sure it would fit against the plywood and then cut the circles into 2½ in. lengths. I glued the pieces onto the substrate using curved clamping cauls (see figure 1 on p. 39).

Cutting parts to shape the lid

I drew a full-size plan view of the lid on a piece of plywood. Actually, I drew two ellipses, one inside the other. The larger, outside line represented the outer edge of the lid. The smaller ellipse inside the first one represented the upper edge of the cove where it meets the flat center portion of the lid (see the top photo on p. 38). Working by eye and with a straightedge, I began experimenting with the layout of the individual segments to be glued to make the lid. The lengths of the pieces were longest near the minor axis and shorter as they approached the tight curves of the major axis.

To achieve the radiating grain pattern I wanted in the finished

lid, I tried different numbers of segments. At first, I tried five pieces in each quadrant of the ellipse, but this resulted in an unsettling V-pattern in the grain where they met. Eventually, I settled on 10 pieces in each quadrant. Having the grain nearly parallel to the edges of each segment looked better. The major and minor axes became my reference lines throughout the project. I made a paper template of one-quarter of the ellipse and divided it into the 10 segments. I transferred the shape of each segment onto the veneered cove stock while carefully aligning the grain. I cut the pieces on a modified cutoff box on the tablesaw (see the photo and drawing above left). I had extra veneered stock in case of error.

Lid pieces are planed to fit, laid like bricks

I had to fit 40 pieces around the lid outline. All were trimmed with a plane on a shooting board to fit correctly (see the photo above right). Beginning with a piece adjacent to a centerline of the ellipse, I planed one edge square and planed the edge of the following piece square to match it. Then I laid both pieces on the plan. Each segment has vertical lines drawn on its sides defining the points where the cove meets the flat top. These lines keep each segment following the ellipse. As I laid each segment on the plan and pressed it against the previous one, the vertical lines had to land directly on the smaller ellipse. If the lines missed the ellipse, planing the edge corrected the angle and solved the problem.

When I had a good dry-fit, I glued and clamped each successive

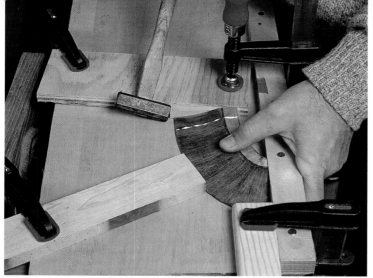

Glue-up is one piece at a time. *Pieces were glued together to form quadrants, or quarters, of the ellipse. These pieces could be glued into halves and, finally, into a completed ellipse.*

Bending forms for the box sides. *Only ³⁄₈ in. thick, the sides of the box are made up of five laminations glued together to form half-elliptical shapes.*

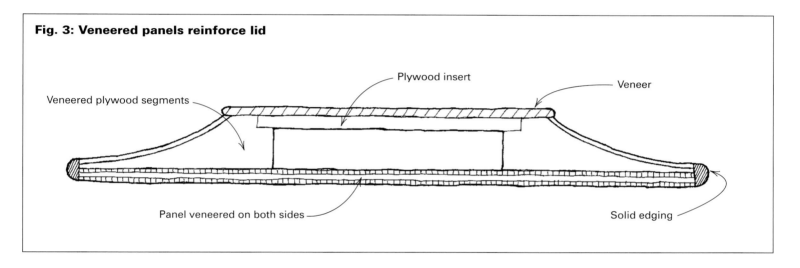

Fig. 3: Veneered panels reinforce lid

Veneered plywood segments

Plywood insert

Veneer

Panel veneered on both sides

Solid edging

piece to the preceding one. I held the work on a flat piece of plywood and clamped each piece between a stop on one side and a block and wedge on the other (see the photo above left). Clamping the block to the plywood, I tapped the wedge between the block and the workpiece for pressure. Secondary blocks kept the work from sliding, and clear packing tape on the plywood prevented accidental gluing of the segments to the plywood.

I flattened the bottom side of the work regularly on sandpaper taped to a piece of plate glass. That kept the lid from getting twisted as I glued up the pieces one at a time. After all four quadrants were glued up, I joined two quadrants to make halves and then two halves to make a whole.

Setting in the top, making the case

Once all segments were glued together, the lid looked like a ring with a hollow center. The lid needed some kind of reinforcement, so I used a router to cut a rabbet around the top inside edge of the ring. That ledge received a plywood insert that tied all the segments together and provided a substrate for the top veneer (see figure 3 above). I glued a thin, veneered panel on the underside of the lid, further strengthening everything. The top veneer went on next, and a pre-bent banding finished the edge.

The ³⁄₈-in.-thick box sides are made of five laminations of material, pre-bent on the heat pipe and glued around a wooden form with a band clamp (see the photo above right). I made two half-

ellipses. Bent laminations usually spring back slightly after they come out of the form, depending on their thickness and the type of glue. But very tight bends will spring forward, becoming more pronounced. This slight tightening didn't affect the fit of the box.

I joined the two halves of the sides and the small ellipse inside the box with loose tenons. Posts on the front and back sides, which improved the appearance, were applied in halves from each side and glued into shallow grooves. The veneered bottom of the box fits into a slot that was plowed out with a slot cutter and bearing on a shaper. I adjusted the depth of the slot by making a bushing from ¼-in. hardboard to fit snugly on the bearing. The bigger the bushing, the shallower the groove.

The base of the box gave me some problems at first. In the original drawing, I found feet attractive. Drawings can be deceptive, though. Once I made a mock-up from rigid foam and looked at the piece from different perspectives, I saw an awkward, cantilevered effect that was unavoidable regardless of how I repositioned the feet. The rounded molding at the bottom of the box worked without the feet, giving visual weight and defining the base. Mock-ups and three-dimensional sketches can reveal oversights before a commitment to solid wood is made (for more on making models, see *FWW* #111, pp. 66-69). The marquetry pattern on the top of the box, by the way, is just a design I drew and liked. ☐

John Gallagher is a furnituremaker living in Fort Bragg, Calif.

Vacuum-Bag Veneering
Using the atmosphere as a low-cost press

by Gordon Merrick

For the first seven years of my career, I thought building with solid hardwoods was the only way to produce real furniture. But the prospects of a lucrative commission from a client who wanted a very ornate period piece opened my eyes to veneering. I was not far into the project, however, before I knew I had entered a whole new area of woodworking with its own set of rules, tenets and Murphy's laws. And all the cumbersome forms required for bending laminations and the plethora of clamps for pressing veneers only gave Murphy more opportunities to intercede. As this project progressed, I was continually impressed by the design freedom possible with veneering. But I was also having numerous problems every time I tried to maintain the alignment of the veneers to each other and to the substratum during glue-up and clamping. So I began trying various presses and clamping systems, searching for more efficient and effective ways to work.

Photo: Ed Chappell

A vacuum-bag veneer press makes it easy to laminate large flat surfaces, like this desktop made by Merrick. Shaping and laminating its curved pedestals was also greatly simplified.

The early days—My first crude veneer press—some crowned 2x4s for battens, a couple of pieces of plywood for cauls and more than 75 clamps—was a nightmare of components and inefficiency. I soon switched to a shop-built 5-ft. by 10-ft. hand-screw veneer press. After investing three weeks and $3,000 in construction, the press solved some of the logistical problems with cauls, clamps and battens, and increased my success rate from 70% to about 80%. But veneers still slipped, causing misalignment and gaps, and I still found occasional air bubbles. And although the press was quicker and easier to use, I spent a lot of time and energy preparing it and cranking down the hand screws and then about 30 minutes recovering from the exertion.

In spite of these shortcomings, I veneered a lot of pieces with this press before I met Darryl Keil, a Freeport, Maine, woodworker who showed me the system he had made for using vacuum pressure to apply veneer. In the vacuum-veneering process, the veneered piece is placed inside a vinyl bag and a vacuum pump exhausts the air from the bag. Atmospheric pressure bears uniformly on all surfaces of the bag, as nature tries to eliminate the vacuum. Sealing the bag and turning on the pump is considerably easier than clamping down a mechanical press, and the even pressure yields greater success than is possible with other systems.

Developing a vacuum system—I was originally introduced to vacuum veneering by Greg Elder's article in *FWW* #56, in which he described the process for making a heavy-vinyl bag and placing the piece to be veneered inside. Once the vacuum is established, the pressure on the veneer can exceed 1 ton per square foot. Although intrigued by the prospects of this perfectly distributed pressure, I was skeptical that such a simple system could really work and so I dismissed the idea as just a pipe dream. But my attitude changed when I met Keil, who was inspired by Elder's article enough to develop his own vacuum press. His enthusiasm and claims of 100% success persuaded me to take a closer look. I was impressed, and Keil's willingness to help me design and build a system convinced me to set up a vacuum-bag press in my shop.

Because of my increasing interest in veneering, we designed the system shown in the left photo on the facing page to meet my then-current demands and future needs. The rack of 2x6s effectively doubled my capabilities and operated in the same amount of space required by the hand-screw press. A manifold with four outlets and a shutoff on each line provides the capacity to add two more bags to the original two-bag system. We also included a mercury switch to control the pump, automatically maintaining a vacuum of 20 in. to 22 in. of mercury (Hg), which translates into an atmospheric pressure of 1,400 lbs. to 1,550 lbs. per square foot.

From *Fine Woodworking* (September 1990) 84:68-70

Above: This two-tier vacuum-bag setup, with a 4-ft. by 8-ft. bag on top and a 5-ft. by 10-ft. bag below, doubles the author's veneering capacity. Clamps and battens seal the bag and a mercury switch on the wall maintains a constant vacuum. Right: The VacuPress can be set up easily and disassembled quickly. Ideal for the small shop with limited production, the quality and durability of this unit make it equally suited to full-time veneering operations.

One drawback to this type of switch, however, is that it must be kept level and perfectly stationary, which means your setup can't be moved easily. With this system, I was able to laminate panels as large as 5 ft. by 10 ft. with just six clamps and two battens holding the end of the bag closed (see the left photo). Whereas loading and achieving full pressure in the screw press required more than 30 minutes, the same job in the vacuum bag is done in less than 10 minutes. Perfectly distributed pressure ensures even contact between veneer and substratum, eliminating bubbles and veneer slippage. The clear vinyl bag lets me check registration of veneer to substratum and even make minor adjustments while the vacuum is being drawn.

And now after pressing more than 10,000 sq. ft. of veneer with this system, I am about to replace it with the VacuPress, shown in the photo at right, which Keil is now producing in quantities. This is the only small-shop commercial system I'm aware of (available from Vacuum Pressing Systems, 10A South St., Freeport, Maine 04032; 207-865-0744). While custom bags can be made, four standard-size bags are available: a 44-in. by 72-in. bag, a 4-ft. by 8-ft. bag, a 4-ft. by 10-ft. bag, and a 4-ft. by 12-ft. bag. While the three large bags open at both ends, the smallest bag has an easy-loading side opening. An optional manifold lets you operate up to three bags from a single pump. The 20-mil vinyl bags are pliable enough to follow any contour when veneering or when forming compound curves, and they stand up to a lot of use. I've been using two bags daily for more than three years.

The VacuPress pump is a compact, self-contained unit that can be set up in your shop or transported to a job site. The only thing you will need to add is a grooved platen of ¾-in.-thick plywood or medium-density fiberboard (MDF). The grooves help draw the vacuum evenly throughout the bag, eliminating pockets of air that might cause the pump to cycle erratically. The pump, rated at ¼ HP, moves 5 cubic feet per minute (CFM) and draws the bag down to its maximum vacuum in less than three minutes. With a properly sealed bag, the pump recycles about every 20 to 30 minutes to maintain a vacuum between 21 in. and 25 in. Hg. This preset range applies more than adequate pressure for all veneering, marquetry and molding processes I've tried.

Although I have a permanent location for my vacuum press, you will appreciate the ease with which the system can be dismantled and stored, especially if you have a small shop. With my setup, I made one platen the recommended maximum size for each bag so that I can press any size piece up to the capacity of the bag. But unless you are veneering a lot of tabletops, you'll probably want to make a smaller 4-ft. by 4-ft. platen. This size makes the system much easier to set up and store, requires less space and handles 90% of your veneering requirements. You could also make a 4-ft. by 8-ft. platen if needed. The same bag can be used for both platens by rolling up and sealing one end to within a few inches of the smaller platen, effectively reducing the size of the bag (see the photo at right on the next page).

Even more than the portability and convenience of this unit, the feature I like best is the bag closure system, shown in the left photo on the next page. Cumbersome battens and clamps are replaced by hook-and-loop fasteners, a clear plastic ⅝-in.-OD rod and a plastic C-channel. The bag is sealed by first folding the open end around the plastic rod and then by pressing the hook-and-loop fasteners together to temporarily hold the bag closed until the C-channel is snapped over the rod.

Working in a vacuum—Although the vacuum system is easy to operate, here are some tips that can improve your success and minimize problems. First, ease the edges and sharp corners of platens, forms or cauls so they don't puncture the bag. As suggested in the operating instructions, I made my platen from plastic-laminated particleboard, which prevents glue squeeze-out from sticking to the platen. But I ripped wider grooves (¼ in.) and spaced them closer (about every 2 in.) than recommended because I found that wider grooves are not as easily blocked by dried glue and that air evacuation is quicker and more complete. Also, a piece of cardboard placed under the bag helps cushion and protect it from any debris.

Even with care, the bag will develop small holes and leaks through normal use, and if they are not patched, they can cause the pump to overwork. Although some leaks are evident either through their hissing sound or from more frequent recycling of the vacuum pump, harder-to-find pinholes can be tracked down by wiping the bag, under vacuum, with a water-soluble dye. The vacuum draws the dye through the bag and reveals the leak. Do this test with just the platen in the bag so you don't stain any veneering projects. Once you locate leaks, patch them with any vinyl-repair kit while the bag is in use so the vacuum holds the patch in place.

When pressing veneers, you will need a caul to protect them from the platen or from the vinyl bag. If veneering both sides of a substratum at once, you will need two cauls. The top caul must be exactly the size of the substratum to ensure proper pressure because a caul that overhangs the substratum may break off or bow up, reducing pressure around the edge of the veneer. This means you may need to cut a new caul for each glue-up. The thickness of the caul is also important and will be determined by the application. A flexible sheet of ⅛-in.-thick bending plywood works best when veneering a curved surface. (Contact Atlantic Plywood Corp., 8 Roessler Road, Woburn, Mass. 01801; 617-933-3830 for your local source.) But for an extremely rippled veneer, you will need a ¾-in.-thick caul that won't conform to the shape of the veneer. The only failure I've had since I started using a vacuum bag came when I glued up badly warped mahogany crotch veneer with a ¼-in. caul on top. Because the ripples in the veneer were stronger than the caul, the caul bent around the veneer rather than pressing it flat, and I ended up with a rippled-veneer panel. Despite the admonitions of my veneer supplier, who said the vacuum bag wouldn't work, I tried again using a ¾-in.-thick caul and had perfect results.

But because of these problems, I veneer one side at a time, with the caul on top of the platen, the veneer placed facedown on the caul and the substratum laid, with the glue-side down, on top of the veneer (see the photo at right). The caul does not need to be the exact size because the substratum distributes the clamping pressure evenly over its entire surface and the veneer is fully supported by the caul below it. To ensure good pressure on the veneered pieces, however, the caul should not be more than 6 in. to 10 in. larger than the substratum. With yellow glue, I leave the panel under pressure for about two hours; but if I need more time during glue-up, I use white glue and leave the panel clamped for at least three hours.

Vacuum veneering allows you to register the veneer to the substratum to within ⅟₃₂-in. tolerances. But to prevent any movement when I slide everything into the bag, I secure the veneer in place on the substratum with a small piece of masking tape. I recently veneered a large oval dining tabletop with 48 pie-shaped segments of Macassar ebony separated by a ⅟₁₆-in. band of inlaid pewter. Even with white glue, my working time was limited to gluing up four sections at a time. And after 12 separate glue-ups, the segments were all perfectly aligned for proper grain and pattern match.

Molding in a bag—Once I became familiar with the machine, I began to experiment with different possibilities, such as all the radius work for the desk in the photo on p. 42. When I was using the hand-screw press, this required constructing a male and female mold and allowing for the thickness of the material being formed between the two molds. For an oval or elliptical shape, building these molds is involved and complex. This prompted me to put just the male form into the bag and bend material over it. I was surprised to find that the uniform atmospheric pressure produced a smooth and perfect radius. In addition to saving significant time in building the molds, the single-mold process makes it easy to add exciting forms to your furniture. Be sure your molds have solid sides to avoid overstretching the bag and have internal ribs to avoid imploding the mold or sucking the platen into the bottom of the mold.

A bendable plywood product, known as wacky wood, wiggle board or bending lauan, works extremely well with the vacuum-forming process. Wacky wood is easily bent even to tight radii, and when two layers of the nominal ⅜-in.-thick material are laminated together with three alternating layers of veneer, a ¾-in.-thick structural panel can be molded into some very interesting shapes. □

Gordon Merrick builds custom furniture in Kennebunkport, Maine.

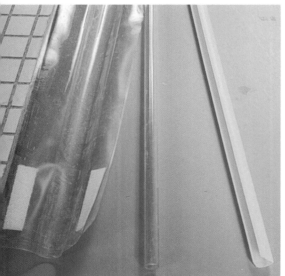

Above: The VacuPress closure system seals the bag securely and quickly. The bag is wrapped around a rod and hook-and-loop fasteners hold it until the C-channel is attached. Right: When laminating one side at a time, Merrick places the veneer on top of the caul, which is usually larger than the applied sheet. Reference marks on the substratum and veneer can be aligned through the bag. For smaller pieces, the bag can be rolled up to within 4 in. of the platen.

Edgebanding
Tools and materials for hiding a panel's edges

by Jack Gavin

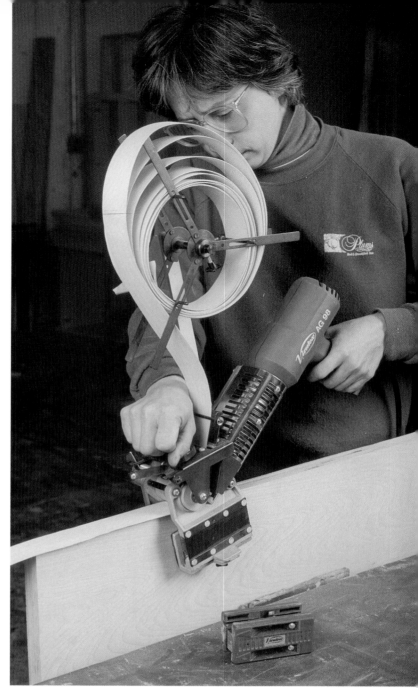

The Virutex edgebander uses hot air to melt the glue on preglued tape. With it, you can apply veneer to panels of almost any size because you move the tool and not the panel. The hand-held Virutex, which costs about $300, can also apply tape to curved edges.

P lywood, fiberboard and particleboard have been a great boon to the modern woodworker. These panel products are solid, easy to handle and relatively inexpensive. They are dimensionally stable and, if stored properly, perfectly flat. Eighteenth-century cabinetmakers would have been ecstatic if they had the opportunity to buy great slabs of material that were jointed, thicknessed, squared, veneered and ready to be cut to any shape. But despite their virtues, panel products all have ugly edges.

Several solutions are possible, but I think edgebanding, a glue-on veneer, is the best. A solid hardwood edge looks great, but making and installing it is very time-consuming. Plastic T-moldings and aluminum edge strips are strictly utilitarian. And nail-on edge moldings have to be filled and sanded. Edgebanding tape, although not a perfect edge treatment, has many advantages. It is faster to apply than any other method of edging, with the possible exception of T-molding. Edgebanding tape is inexpensive, tool outlay to install it can be minimal, and it's available in a great assortment of attractive wood species, as well as in colored plastics and metallics.

You should be aware of several drawbacks to all edgebanding tape. First, it is only as thick as heavy paper and doesn't offer any protection to an edge, as does solid wood. So high-abuse areas should have a heavier, more durable edging. Second, both pressure-sensitive and hot-melt adhesives can be adversely affected by solvents in finishing products. Even though tapes have a solvent-resistant, resin-coated paper backing, solvents can seep into the glue at the tape's joints. You should prime edgebanded panels with a sealer coat of finish, not allowing it to accumulate at the tape's joints. A heavy coat could penetrate and delaminate the tape. Another problem is that you can't do much with a veneered edge but leave it square. You can wrap tape around a bull-nose edge, but it seems to me this would be as much work as using solid wood.

Edgebanding tapes—Tapes are available in several standard widths, $^{13}/_{16}$ in. being the most popular since it is used with $^{3}/_{4}$-in.-thick material. Other common widths include $1^{7}/_{8}$ in., 2 in. and 3 in., but widths up to 12 in. can be ordered from some manufacturers. Wooden edgebanding tape is made by selecting flitches of $^{1}/_{40}$-in.-thick veneer and cutting out imperfections to produce matched 12-in.-wide sheets. These sheets are color matched, spliced into rolls with finger joints and then backed with a resin-impregnated paper before they're sanded. Then the 12-in.-wide roll is slit into narrower widths. To produce preglued tape, hot glue, which is a high-viscosity vinyl-acetate plastic, is applied to the back. Depending on the wood species, preglued veneer tapes cost about 10 cents to 13 cents per foot, and polyvinyl chloride (PVC) tapes cost several cents less.

Depending on the method of application, three different types of edgebanding tape are available. Pressure-sensitive tape, like adhesive tape, is simply pressed on without special tools; preglued

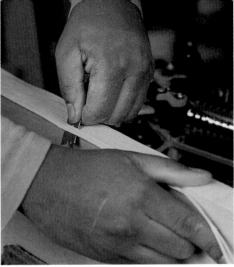

Left: It's simple to apply preglued edge-banding tape with a hot iron that melts the glue. Keep the iron moving and press the tape down with the rounded edge of a piece of wood. Above: After ironing on the tape, it is trimmed with a single-edge razor blade and the corners are lightly sanded.

tape, which has a thin layer of hot glue on the back, is laminated to the edge with a hot iron or edgebander; and non-glued tape is usually applied with an automatic edgebander, which spreads hot glue on the panel edge before it presses on the tape (and some fully automatic machines then trim excess tape from the panel's edges and ends). In each case, it is important that the panel's edge be clean and freshly cut, since dirt or dust on the surface will prevent the tape from sticking properly.

Pressure-sensitive edgebanding tape is the simplest and fastest to apply. You simply peel off its protective backing strip, and then align and rub the tape on the panel edge using the blunted corner of a piece of wood. To finish the corners of the panel, trim the excess tape with a handplane or router and then sand lightly. The tape has an adhesive similar to but stronger than the adhesive on duct tape. Pressure-sensitive tapes have been around longer than preglued tapes, and although the quality of adhesive may vary, the better tapes adhere almost as well as tapes applied with hot glue. The disadvantage of pressure-sensitive tapes is that they cost at least twice as much as preglued or non-glued tapes.

Preglued wood-veneer edgebanding is the most popular type for small shops and non-professionals because it's easy to apply—

Sources of supply

Edgebanding tape is available from:
Canplast Inc., 4797 Couture Blvd., Montreal, Que., Canada H1R 3H7; (514) 327-9555.
Edgemate Division, Westvaco Corp., 333 Closfon Road, Roaring Springs, PA 16673; (800) 458-3761.
Edging Plus, Inc., 103-K Creek Ridge Road, Greensboro, NC 27406; (919) 273-4210.
Flexible Materials, Inc., 11209 Electron Drive, Louisville, KY 40299; (502) 267-7717.
Therm O Web, 112 W. Carpenter Ave., Wheeling, IL 60090; (708) 520-5200.
Woodtape Inc., 11403 120th Ave. N.E., Kirkland, WA 98033; (800) 426-6362.

Edgebanding tools are available from:
Freud, 218 Feld Ave., High Point, NC 27264; (919) 434-3171.
Edgemate Division, Westvaco Corp., 333 Closfon Road, Roaring Springs, PA 16673; (800) 458-3761.
Holz Machinery Corp., 45 Halladay St., Jersey City, NJ 07304; (201) 433-3800.
The Woodworkers' Store, 21801 Industrial Blvd., Rogers, MN 55374-9514; (612) 428-2199.

an excellent job can be done with an electric hot iron and a razor blade (for trimming), as shown in the photos above. Tape usually comes on 250-ft. rolls, and it's available in natural birch, walnut, cherry, mahogany, red and white oak, maple, teak, white ash, pecan and pine. Rolls of flexible plastic edgebanding tape are available in white, almond, gray and black PVC. Some manufacturers will custom make tapes in any wood species or PVC color.

Non-glued tape is designed for automatic edgebanding machines, which have a built-in glue applicator. Without one of these machines, non-glued tapes can be applied with contact cement, hot glue or yellow glue and clamps, but this defeats the purpose of edgebanding. It is supposed to be a simple, fast way to cover panel edges. Non-glued tapes cost about the same as preglued tapes and they come in as many species, colors and sizes, but they are about $\frac{1}{16}$ in. wider.

Applying preglued tape with a hot iron—Although you can apply edgebanding with a variety of equipment, the simplest method is with a hot iron, as shown in the left photo. Turn the iron on "high," place the tape glue-side down on the panel edge and press it on. Allow enough time to melt the glue, several seconds at the most, but don't let the iron linger over any one spot: You can burn the veneer as easily as you can burn a shirt. To adhere the tape to the edge once the glue has melted, use the slightly radiused corner of a wood block and rub the veneer back and forth several times with moderate pressure. If you find any bubbles, simply reheat the veneer with the iron and rub the bubbles out.

After several seconds, the glue will cool and harden. When the glue has cooled, I slice off any excess tape with a single-edge razor blade, as shown in the photo at right, but some people prefer to remove it with a file. Then the corners should be lightly sanded with 120-grit paper. You can use a router with a flush-trimming bit to do the job faster, but the tape may fray and chip when its grain isn't parallel to the edge. I have also seen edgebanding trimmed with a belt sander, but this requires a deft hand to keep from sanding through the veneer on the face of the panel.

The Freud and Virutex edgebanders—Between the hot iron and fully automatic edgebanders are several edgebanding machines, each a little more automated than the next, each a little bit faster and each a bit more expensive. I reviewed two that are somewhat more convenient than but not much faster than a hot iron: the

Freud, shown in the top photo, and the Virutex, shown in the photo on p. 45. The manufacturer's list price for both machines is about $370, although I found them discounted at about $300, and both were easy to set up right from the box. I had to file down the Freud's tape guide, since it scraped glue from the tape before the tape reached the panel's edge. Other than that, both machines worked well once I learned to use them.

And both machines took little time to learn. After several hundred feet of tape I felt comfortable with them, but I still don't consider myself an expert. You must get a "feel" for feed rate, which depends on the heat setting, which in turn depends on your expertise. Applying tape, I averaged 1 ft. in four to six seconds.

I was skeptical that hot air could melt the glue sufficiently. However, the heat in both the Freud and Virutex edgebanders is supplied from adapted Steinel brand adjustable heat guns, which are commonly used to remove paint. And both edgebanders get very hot. In fact, if you linger on one area, you will scorch the veneer. I had to use the Virutex on the lowest setting until I was familiar with it.

The Freud is a stationary machine, mounted on a tabletop, while the Virutex is hand held. Both require preglued tape and have a built-in cutter that trims the tape to length when you finish gluing it to an edge. The Freud works best for panels up to about 2 ft. wide by 3 ft. long. Larger panels are difficult to wrestle through the machine without auxiliary tables to support the weight. Although the Virutex is a bit cumbersome with small pieces, it handles larger panels easily, since you must clamp the panels in a vise and move the machine over the edge. The disadvantage to the Virutex is that the operator must stop and reclamp the panel to tape each edge. This gives the Freud a decided advantage in speed when edging smaller panels. However, an added advantage of the Virutex is its ability to apply tape to curved edges; the Freud can only tape straight edges.

Neither the Freud nor the Virutex automatically trims the excess tape flush with the panel's surfaces, but the Virutex comes with a trimming tool with blades that cut both sides of the tape at once, as shown in the center photo. The idea is good, but the tool tended to tear and chip the tape where the grain wasn't parallel to the tape's edge. Freud doesn't supply a trimming tool.

A fully automatic edgebander—I bought a fully automatic Holz-IDM edgebander for my five-man cabinet shop. The machine is 10 ft. long, weighs 2,500 lbs. and costs almost $20,000. Besides veneer and PVC tapes, this automatic edgebander applies plastic laminate and solid-wood edging up to ½ in. thick. As you feed panels onto a conveyor belt, the machine automatically coats their edges with melted glue before it applies edging material, which is fed from a roll or from a magazine. Then, two saws flush-trim both ends of the edging and two routers cut excess edging flush with the top and bottom panel surfaces. All of this takes about five seconds and the machine edges as fast as I can feed panels into it, all day long.

Now I can apply plastic laminates, as shown in the bottom photo, much faster than with any other method, and I no longer have to wait for contact cement to dry. But the Holz-IDM really earns its keep when thicker wood edging is applied. On a recent job, we built many doors with mahogany veneer on fiberboard cores that were edged with ⅛-in.-thick mahogany on all four edges. It would have taken two men at least four days using yellow glue—clamping, cleaning up squeeze-out, planing, trimming and scraping. The job took three hours with the edgebander, including set-up time. □

Jack Gavin, who owns and operates Gavin Construction in Brooklyn, N.Y., builds custom cabinets and furniture.

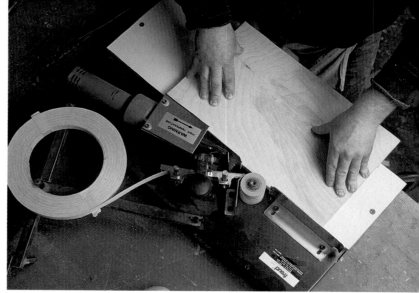

The Freud edgebander can apply preglued tape to panels up to 2 ft. wide by 3 ft. long without table extensions. It melts the tape's glue, automatically applies the tape and has a cutter to trim the tape to length. It sells for about $300.

The Virutex edgebander comes with this trimming tool that cuts both sides of the tape at the same time.

The Holz-IDM is a fully automatic edgebander. It applies hot glue to the panel's edge, presses on either rolled tape or up to ½-in.-thick plastic or wood, saws the banding flush to length and routs it flush with the panel's surface. It sells for about $20,000.

Basics of Vacuum-Bag Veneering

Tips and tricks to make even your first project a success

by David Shath Square

Vacuum-bag veneering is easier with an adaptable setup— *Sectional platens and platforms in this vacuum-veneering work station are supported by sawhorses with dadoed top rails, which* hold interchangeable 2x4 stringers of various lengths. Spring clamps suspended from the ceiling and roller stands at the mouth of the bag make it easy to slip work to be pressed into the bag.

Until recently, I was an advocate of the solid hardwood approach to furniture construction as taught by the cabinet-maker I apprenticed with in the early 1970s. But as it became increasingly difficult to find that perfectly figured rooster-tail walnut, quilted maple or swirl cherry in solid wood, I became more attracted to the exquisite veneers that are readily available. However, I continued to shy away from veneer because of my prejudicial training. Besides, the mechanical veneer presses I had encountered reminded me of unwieldy instruments of torture.

But then I read an article about vacuum veneering by Gordon Merrick (see pp. 42-44). Although skeptical, I was fascinated by the simplicity, flexibility and effectiveness of this system. After some preliminary investigation, I gave into the appeal of veneering and bought a system (see the article on pp. 64-67 for a review of various systems).

Although vacuum veneering is not a complicated process, there are several procedures and techniques that I've learned along the way. These tips, from shop and equipment setup to helpful suggestions about what to try and what to avoid, will help any beginner get off to a smooth start.

Shop layout and equipment setup

I work in a small, one-man shop, and setting up a 4-ft. by 8-ft. table that would handle all my veneering needs was out of the question.

Photos: Charley Robinson

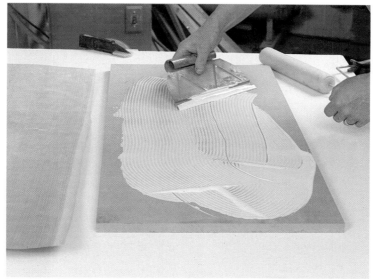

Notched trowel spreads glue uniformly—*The author spreads adhesive with a notched trowel (above) and smooths it with a 9-in.-wide foam roller (below). One ounce of glue per square foot is about right for white polyvinyl acetate on MDF.*

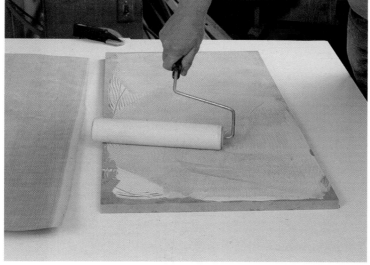

So I designed an adjustable platform system that could be shortened or lengthened to suit various jobs. I generally keep the platform and base in a 4-ft. by 4-ft. mode, as shown in the photo on the facing page, because this handles most veneering needs. The base is constructed of three heavily built sawhorses that have dadoes cut into their top members. A pair of 2x4 stringers rest on edge in these dadoes. They form a joist-like structure to support the melamine sheet that makes up the platform on which the bag and platen rest. To increase the size of the base, I pull the sawhorses farther apart, replace the stringers with longer 2x4s and add another section of melamine.

Whether you are veneering a flat surface or forming a curved panel, a platen is required inside the bag to help draw out all the air and to support the workpiece. I used a ¾-in.-thick melamine panel with a grid of ⅛-in.-wide grooves that are approximately ¼ in. deep and ripped 2 in. apart on the tablesaw. A series of platens can be adjusted along with the platform to suit the size of the work. For most of my work, I use just one section. The setup is easier, and it takes up less of my precious shop space. However, if I'm veneering a large, flat surface, I add more sections side by side in the bag as needed. I also use the smaller platens when pressing a curved panel to allow more room for the bag to envelope the form (see the photo on p. 51).

The lessons of a first project

I kept my initial project, a small table, simple because of my limited experience. I ripped a 29-in. square of medium-density fiberboard (MDF) from a 4-ft. by 8-ft. panel and used an X-Acto knife to slice a 30-in. square of bubinga veneer from a 10-ft. roll. The 30-in.-wide bubinga didn't require any joints.

For this first project, I chose white glue because it had been recommended by a fellow woodworker with a lot of veneering experience. A rule of thumb I've developed is to use approximately 1 oz. of glue per square foot of substrate. However, experience is the best teacher, and you'll soon develop a feel for the correct amount of glue to apply. I poured almost a cup of glue in the middle of the substrate for this table and spread it with a ¹⁄₁₆-in. notched aluminum trowel, as shown in the photos at left. Then I used a 9-in.-wide paint roller with a tight nap to smooth it. The nap left bits of fiber in the glue, and I soon discovered that a cheap foam roller makes a superior spreader. Once I had a uniform film, I placed the bubinga over the substrate, leaving a generous ½-in. overhang all around. I covered the veneer with a layer of 4-mil-thick polyethylene to prevent glue that oozed through the open grain from sticking to the ¼-in.-thick Masonite caul. The caul distributes pressure evenly over the entire veneer surface. (I have since learned that a ¾-in.-thick piece of melamine makes a superior caul because it distributes pressure more evenly, and glue will not adhere to it, eliminating the need for the polyethylene.) With a great deal of difficulty, I single-handedly wrestled the entire sandwich, face side up, into the veneer bag.

I switched on the press, and the 5-cu.-ft.-per minute (CFM) pump exhausted the air from the bag to a vacuum of 25 in. of mercury (Hg), which is about 1,750 lbs. per sq. ft. of pressure, in less than 15 seconds. I was impressed. I was even more impressed when, two hours later, I removed the test piece and examined the bubinga veneer. It was uniformly stuck to the substrate—not a bubble, a wrinkle or a flaw anywhere. A small amount of glue had seeped through the open-grained bubinga, indicating a good initial spread. Too much glue seeping through coats the entire surface of the veneer and too little leaves the surface dry, which means there is insufficient coverage on the substrate.

The only problem was that the ½-in. overhang of veneer had been broken off by the downward pressure of the bag, leaving a ragged edge that had crept onto the finished surface. I corrected this by ripping ⅛ in. off all the edges of the substrate on the tablesaw. I soon realized that placing the substrate in the press veneer side down was a simple way to prevent breaking off the overhang. But I needed a new system to make it easier to load the whole as-

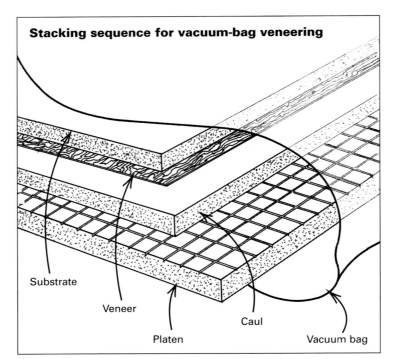

Stacking sequence for vacuum-bag veneering

Substrate

Veneer

Platen

Caul

Vacuum bag

sembly into the vacuum bag.

With this in mind, I devised an efficient system to load a workpiece into the press. On a ¾-in.-thick sheet of melamine that sits on rollers aligned with the mouth of the bag, I place the substrate with the veneer side down. Then I roll the caul-veneer-substrate sandwich into the press shown in the drawing. I use a couple of elastic cords to keep the mouth of the bag open, as shown in the photo on p. 48.

Joining veneers

After my initial success, I was filled with confidence and immediately embarked on a new project. It was a demilune table of Macassar ebony with a top design that required 11 pie-shaped pieces of veneer tightly joined together. I made separate patterns from ¼-in. Masonite, laid each of them on the veneer and then cut out the pie shapes with an X-Acto knife honed on an 8,000-grit waterstone. This yielded an acceptable shape but left a less than perfect edge to join to the next piece in the pattern.

Sand, don't plane, veneer edges for less tearout—An abrasive block is safer to shoot the edges of delicate veneer than a plane. Spray adhesive holds 100-grit garnet paper onto a squared wooden block. The veneer is supported between two pieces of MDF.

I discovered that on straight-grained material, this edge can be perfected by shooting it with a sharp plane, but on highly-figured veneers or pieces that are cut on an angle to the grain, a plane will cause serious tearout. After experimenting with electric routers, jointers and various veneer saws, I made a happy discovery. I cut a 1-in. by 1½-in. piece of hardwood about 12 in. long and glued a strip of 100-grit garnet paper to it (3M's Photo-Mount spray adhesive works well). I shot the edge of the veneer with the sandpaper board by moving it back and forth along the edge of the piece to be jointed, as shown in the photo above. Similar to shooting the edge with a plane, this technique gives excellent results even on Australian silky oak, a veneer that crumbles at the touch of a plane.

I used masking tape on the bottom surface of the veneer to align the eleven wedges of ebony. When I was satisfied with the joints, I flipped the entire pattern over and then applied veneer tape to the top side. Veneer tape is a special, paper-backed tape that re-

quires moistening. It will hold the veneers together without slipping or damaging the veneer and is available from any veneer supplier.

Then I carefully removed the bits of masking tape from the bottom of the veneer. Although it is handy for alignment, masking tape can tear out pieces of wood fiber if not used cautiously. Never run masking tape through the veneer press because it is difficult to remove from the veneer once it has been under about 1,800 lbs. per sq. ft. of pressure. If masking tape accidentally becomes pressed to the veneer, it can be removed by moistening with paint thinner, waiting five minutes and carefully shaving off the softened tape with a cabinet scraper.

Veneer adhesives

I used Titebond aliphatic resin (yellow glue) to glue the ebony to the MDF substrate. It gave excellent results, as did the white polyvinyl acetate (PVA) glue on the bubinga. If I am working on a tabletop or bent lamination that requires a glue with a longer open-time, I use a two-part urea-formaldehyde (Uni-Bond 800, available from Vacuum Pressing Systems, Inc., 553 River Road, Brunswick, Maine 04011; 207-725-0935), which allows for an assembly time of 30 minutes at 70°F. When gluing blond veneers with the tan-colored urea-formaldehyde glue, it is essential to add a lightening agent (also available from Vacuum Pressing Systems) to the mixture; otherwise, bleed-through will stain the veneer permanently.

Although I've used a variety of glues with great success, I've had a problem with hot hide glue. Previous experience with hammer veneering taught me that this material is smelly, messy and difficult to work. It is generally recommended as the glue of choice for applying veneer to the edge of a substrate because it becomes tacky as soon as it cools. In theory, this allows one to brush on a coat, lay the band of veneer along the edge and smooth out the whole mess with a few deft passes of the veneer hammer. In reality, the high water content of the glue causes the veneer to curl like

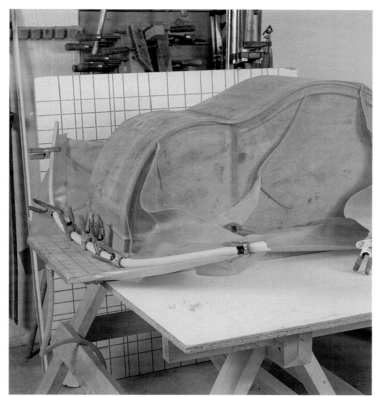

*Curved work must match the vacuum bag size—The circum-
ference of a curved form and the platen should be about 12 in. less
than the bag's, so there's excess bag to follow the contours. A length
of CPVC pipe makes a good closure strip because it's flexible.*

a palsied snake. Moreover, the much touted tackiness usually develops after the band of veneer is stuck to your hammer, your hand or the wall of the shop where you have flung it.

My experience suggests you purchase a can of industrial-quality contact cement (which usually stinks but does the job), and leave the hide glue to the instrumentmakers who use it without difficulty. Although I've heard horror stories of veneer sliding off cabinet sides when glued with contact cement, I've never had any problems when used for small areas, such as edge-banding.

When working with contact cement, I brush a thin coat on both the edge of the substrate and the back of the veneer band. Then I place ⅜-in.-dia. dowels every few inches along the length of the edge. I work carefully from the left to the right, pressing down the veneer with a veneer hammer while gradually removing the dowels, which prevent the band from adhering too quickly or moving out of alignment. The edge of a substrate should be banded before the top and bottom are veneered.

On tables that see daily service, I prefer to add a solid hardwood edge. I use a full-length spline of a material that matches the edge. I cut the mortise in the substrate with a ⅛-in. slot-cutting bit in the router. For speed and convenience, I run the edging through the tablesaw equipped with a carbide-tipped blade that cuts a clean mortise similar in width and depth to that in the substrate. Another alternative that's quick and easy is biscuit-joining the edging to the substrate.

Veneering solid wood and curves

Since I purchased a vacuum bag, my requirements for solid timber have decreased dramatically, although I still use red oak and maple for legs and structural members that require great strength. I find oak particularly good for this job because it is relatively cheap, readily available, takes the veneer well and bends easily where laminated aprons or other curved pieces are needed.

When I veneer a curved leg, I save the waste material from band-sawing the leg to shape to use as a caul. I clean up the kerf marks on the leg and waste piece with a cabinet scraper to ensure a good mate. Then I apply glue and veneer to the leg, cover the veneer with polyethylene and position the waste caul over the veneer. Using this method, I can veneer both the front and the back sides of a curved leg at a single pressing. Moreover, if I am using a glue

with a longer open time, I can prepare and press up to eight legs at once. A carbide-tipped laminate trimmer bit in a router followed by a cabinet scraper is the best way to clean up the veneer overhang once the legs are removed from the press.

I have found, with a little care, the vacuum bag will also accommodate work on large curved surfaces. In this case, a single-part form is sufficient, although a caul of bending plywood is required between the bag and the veneer. Darryl Keil of Vacuum Pressing Systems recommends bending forms be constructed with ¾-in.-thick plywood or particleboard ribs spaced 6 in. on centers with two layers of ⅜-in.-thick bending plywood on top. If the ribs are placed every 3 in., one layer of plywood is sufficient. The ribs should be solid and extend from the top of the form to the platen with a groove cut in the bottom of the form to facilitate air evacuation. The ribs of a bending form should be cross-braced if they are more than 12 in. high. Otherwise, under vacuum, the bag can push in the outside ribs, causing the entire structure, including the workpiece, to deform. It's a good idea to make a test-run under pressure on any new form before it is used in an actual work situation. This allows you to discover any weak points and reinforce them *before* the project is ruined by an inadequately constructed form.

I use ¾-in.-thick spruce plywood (it's cheaper than fir but does the job) when constructing a bending form. I make the form large enough so that the laminates end 2 in. before the form touches the platen to allow enough room for the bag to wrap tightly around the structure.

Some vacuum bags come with a closing system made of stiff, plastic pipe. This system works well when pressing flat surfaces because the bag does not deform. However, to envelope a curved form, the bag must deform dramatically, which can bend or break the closure pipe. The remedy is to purchase an inexpensive length of ½-in.-dia. CPVC water pipe. CPVC pipe is available in plumbing supply shops or home building centers and is more flexible than ordinary PVC. The CPVC pipe is flexible enough to bend with the bag yet has sufficient resilience to resist kinking and breaking, as shown in the photo above. If you also buy a similar length of ¾-in.-dia. CPVC pipe, you can make your own heavy-duty closer strip by cutting it in half on the bandsaw and using it as the outside clip to fit over the small pipe and vinyl.

Sometimes it is necessary to reduce the size of the platen or to construct a specially shaped platen to permit the bag to conform comfortably to the bending form. In this case, it is possible to calculate the size of platen by placing the form on it and measuring the total circumference of both together. This total should be approximately 12 in. less than the interior circumference of the bag. The extra room will allow easy in/out access and keep stress off the seams of the bag. With tall curved forms, it is best to lay the form on its side, and then construct a platen that follows the curve of the form.

As a final word, vacuum veneering has opened a whole new world of woodworking to me. I can now work with beautifully figured exotic woods that I couldn't possibly afford in solid timber. Moreover, I can order the veneers by phone and have them shipped to my home via parcel post at a relatively low cost. The only trips I make to the lumber dealer now are for the readily accessible red oak I use for structural details and the MDF and bending plywood for tabletops and curves. I have never regretted the $800 investment in the vacuum system because it has paid for itself in many ways. But if you can't justify the cost of a commercial system, you should check the story below on making your own vacuum press. □

David Square is a woodworker in Tyndall, Man., Canada.

Make your own vacuum system

by Wayne Locke

I began vacuum-pressing veneers before commercial systems were readily available, so I made my own bag and pump out of necessity. I still make my own because I prefer my connection system, which uses a shop vacuum for fast air evacuation prior to using the vacuum pump. I made my first bags from 10-mil- to 12-mil-thick clear vinyl purchased from fabric stores and put together with Tacky Tape (available from Seal-Tite Systems, Inc., 6357 Reynolds Road, Tyler, Texas 75708; 800-352-4864), an industrial sealant with the consistency of chewed gum that's used as a sealant in the assembly of metal buildings. A more expensive alternative is 883 Vacuum Bag Sealant, a similar product that the Gougeon Brothers, Inc. (100 Patterson Ave., P.O. Box 908, Bay City, Mich. 48707; 517-684-7286) offers for sealing vacuum bags.

Today my main bag is about 4 ft. by 8 ft. It has a clear, 20-mil-thick vinyl top cemented to a thicker gray-vinyl bottom. The gray vinyl is actually a shower pan liner purchased from a plumbing supply house. I glued about a 2-in.-wide joint around three sides of the bag, and then I doubled the wider gray vinyl over the clear and glued it again for a double seal. I made the bottom 6 in. longer than the top and use this excess as a lip for sealing the mouth of the bag. I have never had a joint problem with any bag I've made.

To evacuate air from the bag, I made a manifold of ¾-in.-dia. PVC pipe, as shown in the photo above. The manifold has a leg inside the bag that consists of a 24-in.-long piece of pipe with ¼-in.-dia. holes every 2 in. along one side. This piece connects to a T-fitting. A 6-in.-long pipe connected to the T-fitting exits the bag through a slit in

Shop-built vacuum bag—*Made from 20-mil clear vinyl and shower pan liner, this vacuum bag has held up for several years. The PVC T-fitting connects a vacuum pump to one side and a shop vacuum to the other. The shop vacuum quickly removes most of the air.*

the bag's seam sealed with Tacky Tape. On the outside of the bag, another T-fitting connects the pipe to a ⅜-in.-dia. air hose on one leg and a 6-in.-long piece of capped pipe on the other leg.

The air hose connects my vacuum pump with a quick-connect air fitting for drawing the final vacuum. But first, to quickly remove most of the air in the bag, I slip the 1¼-in.-ID hose of my shop vacuum over the pipe in the other leg after removing the cap. If any realignment is necessary, it's easy enough to remove the hose and move the items in the bag. With everything aligned and most of the air out of the bag, I pull off the vacuum hose and recap that leg. Then my ¼-hp vacuum pump does the rest.

I let the pump run continuously and use a fan timer wired to the motor to control the length of the gluing cycle. I leave curved panels in a vacuum for approximately two

hours to guarantee that the glue has set sufficiently, but for gluing flat faces, less than an hour is fine.

To seal the bag at its mouth, I use a 1¾-in.-thick by 4-in.-wide board a little longer than the width of the bag with a 90° "V" about 1¾ in. wide cut down the length. I made another board to match this V, leaving a ½-in.-wide flat rather than a sharp edge at the apex of the V. In use, the bag is loaded and the lip is folded over the mouth, which is then folded over one or two times. These two boards are then clamped on the fold. A small clamp in the center is usually sufficient because a vacuum bag will almost seal itself if given the chance. □

Wayne Locke is a woodworking teacher at Austin Community College. He is also a designer/builder of furniture, specializing in ecclesiastical pieces, in Austin, Texas.

Curved Panels from a Vacuum Veneer Press

Forms and thin plies make curves a cinch

by Mason Rapaport

***Veneered curves are easier with a vacuum press.** One form and a simple caul are all that are necessary to press a curved, veneered component in a vacuum press. This table, veneered in cherry and walnut, consists of two simple laminations spline-tenoned together.*

O ne of the most used tools in my shop is my vacuum veneer press. In fact, its use in creating veneered curved panels, which are the major components in all of my furniture, is absolutely fundamental. My first encounter with a vacuum press was as an apprentice to woodworker Roger Heitzman in Scotts Valley, Calif., in 1990. At the time, I had no idea how essential to my woodworking that tool would become.

Before the advent of vacuum presses, it was necessary, if you were laminating curved shapes, to build separate male and female forms that both mated very precisely with the layers to be laminated. The whole assembly had to come together as a perfect sandwich, with the forms as bread and the veneers and substrate layers making up the fixings.

But with the vacuum press, I need to build only one form. The vacuum bag and cauls (layers of flexible material that distribute clamping pressure) made from whatever material I'm using as the substrate, take care of the rest. The process can be divided into four main steps: making the form, preparing the substrate and veneer, gluing up and using the vacuum bag to clamp everything together.

Making the form

My bending forms are pretty simple. They consist of sections of particleboard or medium-density fiberboard (MDF) that are bandsawn and routed to the exact profile of the finished curve. These sections, or ribs, are then attached to one another with spacer blocks. The result, as shown in the photo at right, looks sort of like an upside down boat without its hull.

The form needs to be 2 in. or so longer than the final length of the finished lamination. This excess allows you to glue up an oversized piece that is trimmed to fit later. Don't forget to add the excess, or you'll be sorry.

Because all the ribs have to be uniform, the first step is making a master template to cut all the ribs. I start with a scale drawing of the curve I want, and then I enlarge it to full size on a sheet of ¼-in. plywood to make the template. It's important that the template be cut and sanded to a fair curve. Any dips, chips or kinks in the edge of the template will show through on your finished piece.

Trace around your template onto the particleboard or the MDF, and then cut just shy of the line on a bandsaw. Next use a router with a flush-trimming bit, following your template, to get a clean, fair curve. This process ensures that each rib will be identical.

Once the ribs are all cut, take the waste MDF and cut small pieces to use as spacers. Spacing keeps the weight of the form down but maintains sufficient rigidity so that the form will not deflect under pressure. To assemble the form, I use yellow glue, along with nails or screws, and a good combination square to make sure the form goes together square. The form should be as wide as the final piece, plus an inch or so on either side to allow for final, accurate trimming.

Preparing substrate

I use ⅛-in. Italian bending poplar or 1.5mm (about 1⁄16 in.) Finland birch for the substrate, depending on the radius of the curve I'm bending. The Italian poplar will bend to a radius of about 2⅛ in.; the 1⁄16-in. birch will bend to about 1 in. radius. When rough-cutting thin sheets, use an auxiliary fence or some other means to prevent the sheets from sliding under the tablesaw fence. Remember to cut the sheets of plywood slightly oversize; final trimming takes place after the piece comes out of the press. Bending plywoods are available in sizes down to .4 mm (about 1⁄64 in.) from specialty plywood dealers, such as Harbor Sales (1401 Russell St., Baltimore, Md. 21230; 800-345-1712).

Preparing the veneer

If one sheet of face veneer will do the job, I just rough-cut it slightly oversize with a sharp razor knife or veneer saw. But if the face veneer has to consist of several pieces, things get a little more complicated. Their

Bending forms are easy to make. Using yellow glue and nails (or screws), you can assemble a form quickly from ribs of medium-density fiberboard (MDF). Use a combination square to make sure all the ribs are aligned.

Laminate trimmer and flush-trimming bit joint veneers. To joint veneers for wide panels, the author uses a laminate trimmer (a small router) and a bearing-guided flush-trimming bit.

edges have to be precisely jointed. To joint two sheets of veneer, I just sandwich them between two boards; the edge of the bottom board must be jointed and stick out ever so slightly (say, 1⁄32 in.) beyond the top board. When clamped together with both pieces of veneer between and their edges sticking out past the bottom board, jointing is a simple matter of routing. With a bearing-guided, flush-trimming bit, make a pass down the board, and that's that (see the bottom photo on this page).

Use veneer tape (a water-activated adhesive tape available from veneer suppliers) to tape these jointed veneers together. Tape them along the seam on the face side. Then use a hot iron on the veneer tape to dry the tape and to shrink it a bit, so the joint between the veneer sheets is very tight. The veneer will warp a bit from the iron's dry heat but not enough to matter when it goes into the vacuum press.

The last thing to do before glue-up is to mark each ply and sheet of veneer on one edge with a tick mark at the center to help align the layers on the form.

Photos except where noted: Vincent Laurence

Glue-up

Next I glue up the stack of plies and veneer using a urea-formaldehyde or plastic-resin glue. I use these glues because of their longer open times compared to yellow glue and because they don't creep. The glue I use most often, Unibond 800 (available from Vacuum Pressing Systems, 553 River Road, Brunswick, Maine 04011; 207-725-0935), also is available in different colors and can be dyed to make gluelines or squeeze-out less obvious. Unibond cleans up with warm water—not an easy thing to do with plastic-resin glues. And set-up time can be modified by the application of heat and by the ratio of resin to hardener you use.

Apply either of these types of glue with a thin, foam-covered roller (available at most hardware and paint stores). A thin, even coat on one of the two surfaces will create a strong glue bond (see the top photo on this page). Finally, after you've glued and stacked all the layers, use the tick marks on the veneer and substrate to

Foam roller spreads urea formaldehyde or plastic-resin glues easily. These two types of glue have longer set times than white or yellow glues, so they're better for most veneer work. A thin, even layer of glue on one of the surfaces is sufficient.

Make sure the bag isn't pinched. Check that the bag isn't caught between layers of the lamination, the form or the platen. There should be no air pockets between the bag and the lamination, which would mean a weak bond in that spot.

From *Fine Woodworking* (January 1995) 110:82-85

align the stock correctly. Use masking tape to hold the stack together at the center on both sides.

Into the vacuum bag

Inside the vacuum bag, I use a melamine platen (a large flat plate on which something is pressed). I cut ⅛-in.-wide, ⅛-in.-deep grooves with a tablesaw to make a grid of 6-in. squares on the platen, as recommended by the manufacturer. The platen is 2 in. to 4 in. larger than the base of the form, so there's plenty of bag to wrap around the form. The form goes in the bag and on the platen. I keep the form as close to the opening as possible to make it easier to put the lamination into the bag. I also roll up the unused end of the bag. That way, the vacuum pump doesn't have to work as hard at evacuating air from the bag initially, and the pump cycles-on less often while the glue sets.

Now I put the laminations into the bag with waxed or paper-wrapped cauls top and bottom to ensure even pressure over

the entire lamination. The edges of the form and of the cauls are rounded over, so they don't puncture the bag. I usually duct-tape the whole lamination to the form at a center point I've marked on the form. The masking tape that I put on earlier over the center mark of the lamination locates its center. The duct tape keeps the lamination in place, but it still allows the plies to slide by each other as they get squished against the form.

Once I've closed the bag and started to pump out the air, I move quickly. It's important to make sure the bag isn't pinched between the form and platen, between lamination and form or between layers of the lamination itself. If you do pinch the bag, you'll end up with a void in the lamination and a bump on its surface.

It's also essential to check that the bag is bearing against the entire lamination, that it isn't hung up anywhere (preventing it from contacting the lamination) and that the bag has been evacuated completely (see the bottom photo). Sometimes air pockets remain because the bag has closed off any exit channels, which can keep layers of the lamination from bonding. If I see any gaps between plies at the edges, I'll turn off the vacuum pump, open the bag, let some air in, close the bag and start evacuating it again, taking more care to see that the bag seats flush against the entire lamination.

Electric blanket speeds drying

To speed the glue-cure time once the lamination is under pressure, place an electric blanket, set on high, over the bag. This can reduce the cure time of the Unibond from about four hours to just over an hour. Electric blankets weren't designed to be folded over a plastic bag, though, so don't leave the blanket on unattended.

I leave my glue-mixing stick underneath the blanket on top of the vacuum bag, and I set an inexpensive plastic thermometer next to it. By knowing the temperature just outside the bag and comparing this information with that provided by the manufacturer of the adhesive, I can get a rough idea of how long before the glue will be cured; then I can turn off the blanket and the vacuum pump. The reason for keeping the glue-mixing stick there is just to play it safe. It will show me for certain when the glue has cured. When the thin film of adhesive that remains on the mixing stick has turned brittle and dry, then the lamination is ready. □

Mason Rapaport designs and builds furniture in Easthampton, Mass.

Curves to fit any style

by Vincent Laurence

One of the great things about learning how to make curved, veneered panels is that the technique can be applied to many different kinds of furniture. As the pieces on this page show, curved panels faced with veneer can be used on everything from a Federal-style demilune table (see the top photo) to an Art Deco television cabinet (see the center photo). No matter what the style, the veneering process is the same.

Using a vacuum bag to press the veneer onto its substrate is more than versatile. It's also simple. Vacuum pressing means that you'll only need one form, not two, to get the right shape. The technique allows you to exert even pressure over the entire panel, making for a strong, reliable bond between the veneer and the substrate. The results can be gratifying—no matter what kind of furniture you like to make. □

Vincent Laurence is an associate editor for FWW.

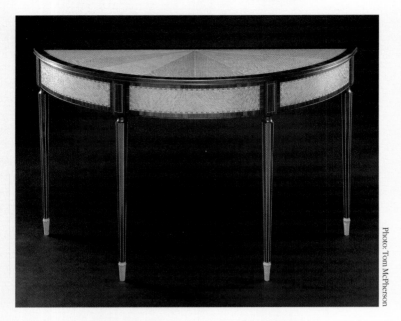

Photo: Tom McPherson

Bending plywood hides beneath exotic veneers on this Federal-style demilune table made by Daryl Keil of Brunswick, Maine. Keil used six layers of ⅛-in. Italian poplar bending plywood for the substrate of the front panels. The sunburst pattern in the top and the rectangular centers of the aprons are Australian lacewood. East Indian rosewood was used for the legs, the crossbanding around the panels and for the moldings.

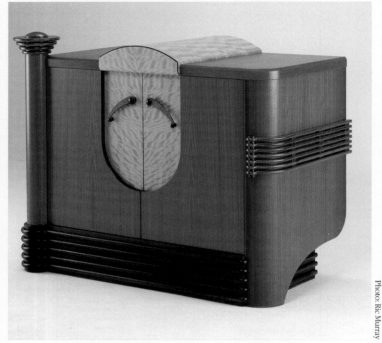

Photo: Ric Murray

Inspired by Art Deco radios of the '30s and '40s, Steven Turino made this TV/VCR cabinet. He used particleboard forms for all the curved sections of his cabinet and used Italian bending poplar as the substrate for the curves and medium-density fiberboard (MDF) as the substrate for the flat sections. The cabinet is padauk with African satinwood in the center and Ebon-X, an ebony substitute, for the base. The trim details on the side and at the top of the column are MDF with a crackle lacquer finish.

Photo: courtesy of Peter Joseph Gallery

Simple lines and stunning wood are the strengths of this Ruhlmann-inspired Macassar ebony sideboard. Rhode Island furnituremaker Timothy S. Philbrick laminated the substrate for the front of the sideboard with two layers of ¼-in. Appleply, a voidless American-made plywood.

The author peels birch bark from the log with a 2-in. slick. The board lying behind him can be used to help hold the bark out of the way as the work progresses.

Veneering with Birch Bark

A *natural way to add a decorative touch*

by Dick Sellew

I've always enjoyed the natural beauty of the birch trees that grow in abundance on my father's 100-acre lot in southwestern Massachusetts. The contrast of the dark streaks on the lighter background and the texture of the bark itself is so intriguing that I wanted to incorporate these features in my work. The similarities between the flexible bark and veneer inspired my first efforts: I veneered the aprons on a Shaker-style table and found the effect very appealing. Flush with success, I veneered a folding screen, but the ostentatious bark on this scale was overpowering.

As a result of these experiments, I use small splashes of bark to accent and brighten simple designs, like the display tables shown in the photo at right on the following page and discussed in the sidebar on p. 59. I also played with color by using various hardwoods or tints and dyes, and found that the bark's neutral color goes well with almost everything.

Finding and harvesting birch bark—One of the most enjoyable aspects of working with the bark is tramping through the woods looking for the perfect birch tree. Indians harvested bark for their canoes in the spring or fall, when the sap is running and the trees are easier to skin. I'm not excited about taking bark off living trees; it reminds me a little of elephant hunters seeking the tusks. But I enjoy roaming the woods for dead birch trees and there is a certain satisfaction in knowing that an otherwise lost resource will find a continuing life in one of my projects. Stripping a dead tree is also easier than a live tree, because often the trunk has shrunk, leaving the bark loose and manageable. Also, I have found the bark to be looser in late winter or early spring than in the hot and humid summer. To avoid a lot of strenuous hauling, I debark the logs where I find them. Other than a chainsaw, all you need is a razor knife, a 2-in.-wide slick chisel and a ¾-in. board, roughly

6 in. wide by 24 in. long, beveled along one edge. To further simplify the equipment requirements, you can substitute a bucksaw and a lot of energy for the chainsaw.

I look for a birch tree that has enough clear bark to cover the individual pieces of a project. Because birch bark has many layers, surface defects like sloughy bark, mold and other growth can be removed easily, but branch protrusions and other defects that penetrate the bark should be avoided. You can glue up sections of the bark for larger panels, but unlike regular veneer, the seams will generally show and it would be almost impossible to match patterns for making repairs. If I find a prime tree with lots of clear bark, I try to get as large a piece as possible. However, the larger skins are also more difficult to handle and apply as veneer. Designing projects with only small areas of bark makes your quest much easier because almost any dead tree will do.

If the birch tree I select is still standing, I first cut it down with my chainsaw and then section it to yield the largest pieces of clear bark. With the razor knife, slit the bark the length of the log section, and then begin working the 2-in.-wide slick between the bark and the sapwood along the length of the slit. Grasp the edge of the bark with your free hand and continue working around the log with the slick to free the bark, as shown above. Once you get one-third to one-half of the way around the log, or if the bark starts to split, use the bevel-edge board for holding and pushing the bark back as you continue to peel it away with the slick. If the bark is particularly difficult to remove, find another dead tree to debark, leaving the first tree for another day.

When I arrive back at my shop, I flatten the bark by moistening its inside face, laying it on a flat surface and then weighting it down under a piece of plywood to dry overnight. The next day, I clean both faces of the bark with a standard 1-in.-wide paint scraper to

From *Fine Woodworking* (July 1990) 83:57-59

Above: After contact-cementing the bark veneer to the leg, the excess layers are peeled away to leave a single layer of paper-thin veneer. Below: The author blows off loose and damaged bark with compressed air at 80 psi. Clear sections of bark large enough to cover the aprons and top can then be selected.

The plain lines of these display tables make a perfect stage for showing off the natural beauty of the unusual birch-bark veneer that accents the top, aprons and feet.

remove dirt, mushrooms and other protrusions that would damage the bark during clamping. Although you should exercise some care in this operation, don't be overly concerned about marring the bark because removing the sloughy outer layers with blasts of compressed air at 80 psi, as shown in the bottom, left photo, will also remove minor defects. The bark is ready for veneering when the air blasts no longer lift loose layers. As an alternative to compressed air, you can apply 2-in.-wide masking tape to the face of the bark. When the tape is removed, it will pull away loose bark. However, this method is slow going and will require several taping applications.

Applying birch-bark veneer—There are other differences between birch bark and regular veneer besides matching patterns and hiding joints. Because the bark-veneered panels are small, the stable man-made core materials can overcome any tendency to warp when veneered on only one face. For anything larger than a square foot, however, I recommend laminating the opposite face with any 1/28-in.- or 1/32-in.-thick veneer so that the panel's construction remains balanced. Also, you can apply the bark veneer before cutting your pieces to final size. If I veneer after the panel is sized, I allow the birch bark to overhang the backing panel and then I trim the bark with a flush-trimming bit in my router. However, the bark mars very easily and cannot be sanded, so you must handle it with care throughout the process. One benefit of the delicately layered bark is that minor blemishes can be repaired by blowing off a few more layers.

Using your backing panels as templates, select and cut the birch bark, allowing about 1/8-in. overhang on all sides. Roll or spread a thin, even coat of yellow glue on the back of the bark to ensure good adhesion without a lot of squeeze-out and then position the bark on the backing panels. I tape the bark to keep it from slipping out of position and clamp the panels in pairs, using 3/4-in. plywood on top and bottom as pads and wax paper between the layers to keep them from being glued together accidentally. For larger panels, you will need heavier cauls and battens to evenly distribute the clamping pressure. Make sure there is no debris on the cauls or panels, as this could damage the bark before clamping the layers together. I like to let these veneered panels dry at least six hours

and preferably overnight. When the clamps are removed, I again blast the bark with 80 psi of air to remove any more loose material.

Detail work, such as on the bottoms of the legs of the display table in the photo at right, is best done by laminating the bark directly to the piece. I used to inlay this detail, but because of the variability in thickness of the birch bark, it was a time-consuming process and it was impossible to get the veneer flush with the surface. Now I contact-cement a piece of bark to the surface and peel away the extra layers, leaving a single thickness of paper-thin bark; this method is quicker and yields more consistent results.

Finish-sand the piece before veneering and assembling, as this single layer is easily damaged. When veneering the feet of table legs or when accenting a similar piece, I use a hardboard template to cut strips of bark to size. After covering the area with contact cement, I apply the bark and fix it with firm pressure from a veneer roller to ensure good contact. Trim the bark to the edge of the piece with a safety razor blade and then use the blade to lift up a corner of the extra bark and pull it away (see the top, left photo). Turn the piece and repeat this procedure until all sides are done.

Applying a finish—As I mentioned earlier, I think the birch bark looks good with a variety of colors, so don't be afraid to experiment with tints, stains and dyes. For a protective finish, however, I prefer Sherwin-Williams Sher-Wood, a moisture-resistant lacquer with a medium sheen. Before finishing, touch up with 120-grit sandpaper, but be sure to avoid the birch bark. Then spray on the first sealer coat. I let this coat dry an hour and then test the adhesion of the birch bark with a blast from the air compressor. If there is any sloughing at this point, a lighter-color lower layer of bark will be revealed. However, another light coat of Sher-Wood on the damaged area will usually blend it in with the rest of the piece. Sand between coats, avoiding the bark, and apply two more coats per the instructions on the can. The final coat can be left as is, waxed, or polished with wool lube or rubbing compound to the desired sheen. □

Dick Sellew is a furnituremaker in New Marlboro, Mass.

Making a display table

I designed this display table with simple lines to complement the more intricate pattern of the birch-bark accents on the aprons, top and feet. By using sliding tables on my tablesaw to cut all the parts, construction goes very quickly. I used biscuits to join the tapered legs to the bark-veneered plywood aprons and to join the mitered frame to the bark-veneered top. A piece of glass recessed into the top frame protects the birch bark, and metal tabletop fasteners secure the assembled top to the base.

Shaping the legs: I use three shopmade sliding tables with a variety of guides and stops to taper the legs, cut the compound angles for the top and bottom of the legs, cut the angled sides of the aprons, and miter the top edgebanding. With these setups, I perform repeated operations easily and accurately; I can then quickly assemble the display table with biscuit joints, as shown in the drawing at right.

I begin by dimensioning the leg stock as shown and then arranging the four legs for the most pleasing grain and color match. Next, I number each leg and mark the outside faces for reference when cutting and assembling the table. Tilt the tablesaw blade to 5° and with a 5° angle block on the sliding table, cut off the top and bottom ends of the legs. To cut the top of each leg, the outside faces of the leg should be against the fence and the table, but for the bottom, these faces should be away from the fence and table. Beginning 10 in. down from the top, I taper both inside faces of the legs, from 1½ in. at the top to ¾ in. at the bottom, on an extra-long sliding table with a tapered fence. A regular taper jig and the standard tablesaw fence can also be used. Clean up the sawmarks with a light pass on the jointer or with a handplane.

Assembling the base: The sides of the aprons are mitered at 5°, thereby splaying the legs for a lighter appearance and a stable base. After veneering the core material, flush-trim the overhanging bark with a router (see the main article). I usually veneer oversize blanks and then cut them to the sizes given in the drawing on a sliding table, using a 5°-angle block on the left side for the first cut and a 10°-angle block on the right side to compensate for the 5° angle already cut. A ¼-in.-deep sawkerf, located ½ in. down from the top edge of the apron, receives the tabletop fasteners (available from The Woodworkers' Store, 21801 Industrial Blvd., Rogers, Minn. 55374-9514; 612-428-2199) that hold the top to the base.

I join the aprons to the legs with two #10 biscuits at each joint, recessing each apron ¼ in. from the face of the legs. Biscuits were developed specifically for manufactured sheet goods and they provide a reasonably secure joint between man-made panels or between panels and solid stock. Additionally, biscuits are great in production situations because they are quick and easy to use. (See *FWW* #76, pp. 60-64, for more on biscuit joiners.)

Before gluing up the base, use the previously drawn reference marks to ensure that the legs are in the appropriate position, and have clamps and pads close at hand. To ease the burden of holding clamps, pads, legs and an apron all at the same time, I make special clamping pads by sandwiching two pieces of ½x1½x8 scraps between two pieces of 24-in.-long duct tape, with the scraps at each end of the tape. Spread the glue evenly on the sides of the biscuit and the slots, as well as on the edge of the apron and on the mating face of the leg. Glue two leg-apron units, aligning the top of the apron with the top of the legs. The special clamping pad is then laid across the top of the leg-apron unit, with the wood scraps hanging down the sides of the legs ready for clamps. After clamping, check that the unit is square and flat, and clean up squeeze-out with a damp rag, rubbing gently to avoid damaging the bark. When the glue has dried, complete the base by gluing these two units to the remaining aprons.

Topping it off: The top edgebanding is mitered on a sliding table and biscuit-joined to the veneered plywood top. By aligning the bottom of the edgebanding with the bottom of the plywood top, a recess is created for plate glass that protects the bark from wear and tear. A full ⅞-in.-thick top looks heavy on this small table; so I bevel the underside of the edgebanding on the tablesaw to form a ¼-in.-thick edge. A light touch with a belt sander removes sawkerfs, and you're ready for finishing as discussed in the main article. *—D.S.*

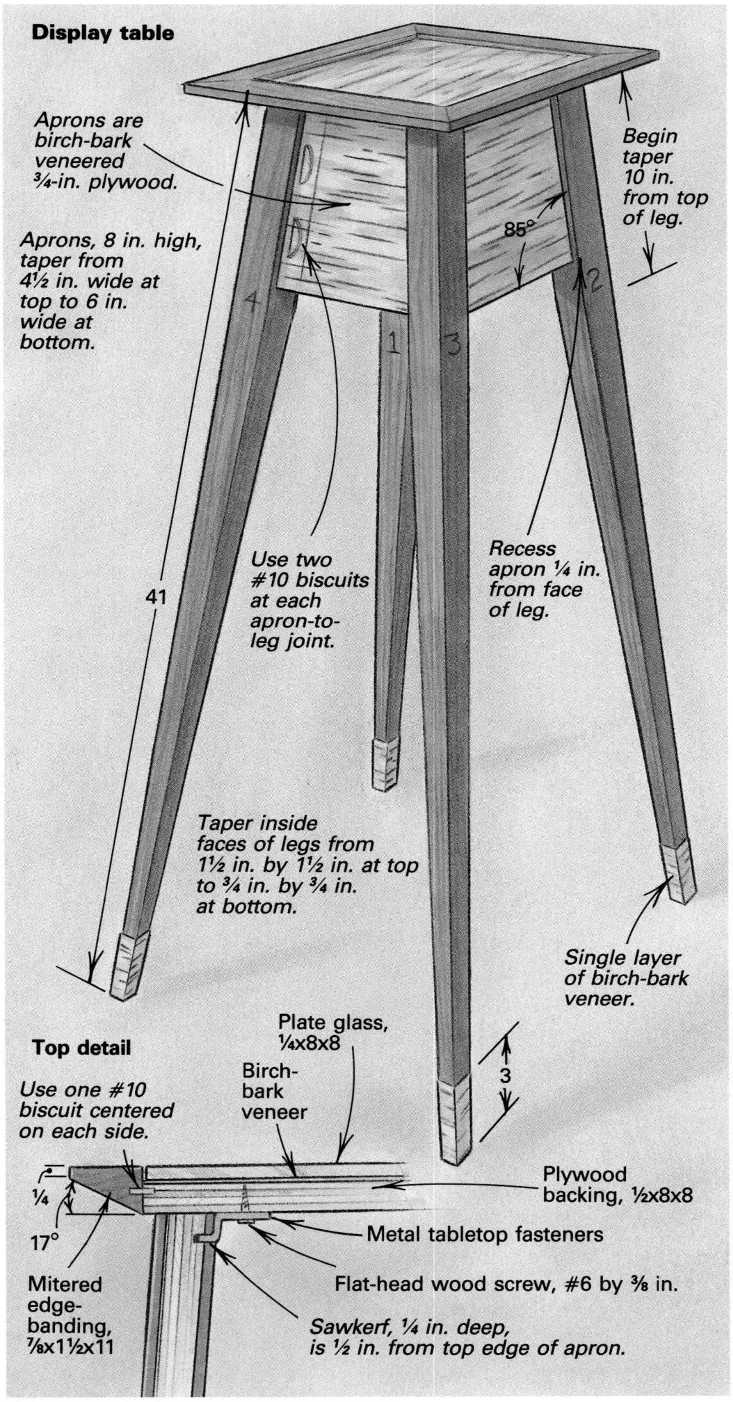

Display table
Aprons are birch-bark veneered ¾-in. plywood.
Aprons, 8 in. high, taper from 4½ in. wide at top to 6 in. wide at bottom.
Begin taper 10 in. from top of leg.
85°
4
1
3
2
41
Use two #10 biscuits at each apron-to-leg joint.
Recess apron ¼ in. from face of leg.
Taper inside faces of legs from 1½ in. by 1½ in. at top to ¾ in. by ¾ in. at bottom.
Single layer of birch-bark veneer.
3
Top detail
Use one #10 biscuit centered on each side.
Plate glass, ¼x8x8
Birch-bark veneer
Plywood backing, ½x8x8
¼
17°
Metal tabletop fasteners
Mitered edge-banding, ⅞x1½x11
Flat-head wood screw, #6 by ⅜ in.
Sawkerf, ¼ in. deep, is ½ in. from top edge of apron.

Drawing: Bob La Pointe

Making a Veneered Game Cabinet

A journeyman's exam piece to test your skill

by Norbert Heinold

This veneered game cabinet was part of the author's journeyman's exam. Building it not only provides attractive and flexible storage for a variety of games, but it also provides lessons in a variety of veneering techniques with several different core materials.

While electronic games are currently all the rage, traditional pastimes like chess, checkers and backgammon are still very popular. These games have lots of pieces, however, that become dust collectors or are easily lost unless you have a good way to store them. A game chest or cabinet has been a practical and beautiful solution to these problems for centuries. The inlaid decorations on the cabinet shown here add some fun to the piece, and challenge the woodworker's skill.

This game cabinet is the culmination of my three-year apprenticeship at Werkstaetten Knorr, a workshop in Wuppertal, Germany. As part of my journeyman examination, I had to design and build a cabinet with doors and at least one dovetailed drawer; so I developed the veneered game cabinet shown in figure 2 on p. 63. Veneering has many advantages over solid-wood construction. First, using dimensionally stable core materials eliminates wood-movement problems. And veneers are available in species that might otherwise be prohibitively expensive, are easily stored and can be made into panels of any size. But the main reason I favor veneers is they allow for a design freedom that is impossible to achieve with solid woods.

Because the construction of the game cabinet is relatively simple, here I'll concentrate primarily on veneering techniques rather than on joinery. The carcase is ¾-in. lumbercore plywood, edged in solid mahogany, and veneered on the outside with mahogany and on the inside with maple, as shown in figure 2. The mitered corners are reinforced with special L-shape plastic angles; I haven't found these in the United States, but instead you can use plastic miter dowels (available from The Woodworkers' Store, 21801 Industrial Blvd., Rogers, Minn. 55374-9514; 612-428-2899). The parti-

tions and top and bottom shelves are doweled in place, but the other three shelves are adjustable to provide flexible storage for board games. To make the drawers for game pieces and cards, I screwed an inlaid and veneered front to dovetailed maple boxes, as shown in figure 2 on p. 63. I picked ¾-in. particleboard as the core material for the doors because greater dimensional stability is particularly important for inlaid veneers. The particleboard is edgebanded with solid mahogany and veneered on both sides with book-matched mahogany. Ledger strips attached to the inside of the doors store two veneered game boards.

Some veneering basics—Veneering requires few special tools: an X-Acto knife, a veneer saw, a paint roller for spreading glue and most importantly, a method for applying even pressure over a large surface. Hot-press veneering provides a solid, durable, moisture-resistant bond and is my favorite method, but the high cost of a hot press (as much as $40,000) puts this technique out of reach for the average woodworker. Cold pressing remains the most reasonable alternative for the home woodworker. The most common method of cold-pressing veneers, and the one I'll discuss here, is with clamps, press plates and cauls, which distribute clamping pressure across the entire veneer, as shown in figure 1 on the facing page. Another cold-pressing method gaining popularity is vacuum veneering (see the articles on pp. 42-44 and pp. 48-52).

Any veneer project starts with selecting and preparing the core material. Furniture-grade particleboard or preferably medium-density fiberboard (MDF) offers an extremely stable base for veneer, but both are heavy. Although plywood is a lighter yet still stable material,

From *Fine Woodworking* (July 1990) 83:68-71

it tends to warp or cup unless held in place by carcase joinery. Whatever core material you choose, the edges must be banded. Edgebanding not only dresses up the raw core material, but also provides a solid surface for joining, hanging hinges, machining details or easing the veneered corners without fear of sanding through to the core. Often, veneer suppliers can provide solid stock from the same tree as the veneer so the solid edgebanding matches the veneered faces. The edgebanding should be just wide enough to accommodate the desired edge treatment. The wider the edgebanding, the more it will react to moisture changes, while the man-made core material remains stable. This may result in the glue joint between the edgebanding and the core material telegraphing through the veneer. After I glue on the solid edgebanding, I usually wait two to three days to allow for any minor wood movement before planing the edgebanding flush to the core material and veneering the faces.

Because veneers are so thin, usually ranging from 1/16 in. to 1/32 in. thick, it is easy to store a large quantity in a small space. But proper storage is important. Lay the veneer sheets out flat so they are fully supported with no overhang. Keep the sheets away from direct sunlight, which can fade the woods. If possible, the veneer should be kept at a temperature of 60°F to 70°F and a humidity of about 80%. If you live in a dry area, wrap the veneer in plastic to retain moisture and keep it clean. However, if the veneer is too dry or cracked, sprinkle water on each sheet and put it in a cold press or on a cement floor weighted down under boards for at least six hours and preferably overnight. After the sheets are flat and dry, tape the cracks and secure the ends with veneer tape to prevent further cracking. For greater stability when using a plywood core, the veneer grain must be perpendicular to the plywood grain.

A major principle in veneering is that core materials must always be veneered equally on both sides or else each face will react to moisture differently and the piece will warp. Generally, the backing veneer can be an easily worked species such as mahogany, but it should be the same thickness as the show veneer to maintain structural balance. Bird's-eye maple veneer, however, should be backed by bird's-eye maple, even if it will not show, because this veneer is strong enough to bend more easily worked species.

Applying veneers—Before beginning a veneering project, you should be well organized, have a clean working surface, and prepare the core material and veneers, including marking each piece so you know exactly where it goes. A felt-tip marker works well to mark the core material, but chalk is better on the veneers and is easier to remove. All surfaces have to be sanded, clean and dry, and you should have plenty of glue and clamps. A shopmade press, like that shown in figure 1, can greatly reduce the problems of managing the numerous pieces of plywood, particleboard, battens, cauls and clamps. MDF on the face of the cauls provides a very stable and perfectly flat surface. Plastic laminate or heavily waxed tempered hardboard makes good press plates that won't stick to the veneer and that are easily cleaned of glue that might squeeze through the porous veneer.

Begin the actual veneering process by placing the bottom caul on a work surface or bench so you can clamp along both the front and back sides. Lay the bottom press plate on the caul and then lay the backing veneer facedown on the bottom press plate. Make sure no debris is stuck to the cauls, press plates, veneers or core material that might mar the finished surface. With a paint roller, apply a thin, even coat of white glue to one side of the core. Experience is the only way to learn how much glue is needed, as requirements will vary with each material and veneer. But you don't want so much glue that it squeezes out around the edges and through the veneer, creating a mess that requires considerable scraping and sanding to clean up. Then, place the core, glued-side down, on top

of the backing veneer. After rolling a thin, even coat of glue on the exposed side of the core, complete the veneer "sandwich" by adding the face veneer, the top press plate and finally the top caul. Begin applying clamp pressure from the center of the panel to the outer edges, to avoid trapping glue in the center and causing bubbles in the finished surface. Leave the panel clamped for two to four hours, or longer depending on humidity and temperature. Higher temperatures cause the glue to set more quickly. Conversely, higher humidity lengthens the setting period by increasing the moisture content of the wood, and it inhibits glue penetration. I leave some veneers, such as inlays, clamped for eight hours or more. Once the panels come out of the press, I trim the overhanging veneer with a knife, a saw or just a sanding block with 80-grit to 100-grit paper.

It is common for the veneer to slip slightly on the core as the clamps are tightened. Because the veneers are cut about 1/2 in. oversize on each side, this is usually of little consequence. However, if grain orientation or positioning is important, as with the game boards, I prevent veneer slippage by gluing 1/4x1/4x7 pine positioning blocks on each corner, as shown in figure 1 below.

Inlaying veneers—I really enjoy inlaying designs and decorations in my projects. Not only do they add interest and detail, as shown in the photos on the following page, but they can provide information about the piece. The playing card symbols on the doors of my game cabinet and the game pieces on the drawer fronts, for example, tell what's inside.

To inlay a pattern, draw the design on the background veneer, or on a piece of paper and then tape the design to the veneer. Holding the X-Acto knife at 90°, cut the pattern for the inlay from the background. Choosing the right color and pattern for the inlay from the dizzying selection of domestic and exotic veneers that is available can take longer than the actual cutting. But attention to detail here is important to the overall success of the piece.

The fruit-wood veneers, like cherry, pear, plum and apple, are best for beginners because they are easy to work. Walnut and maple

Fig. 1: Shopmade veneer press

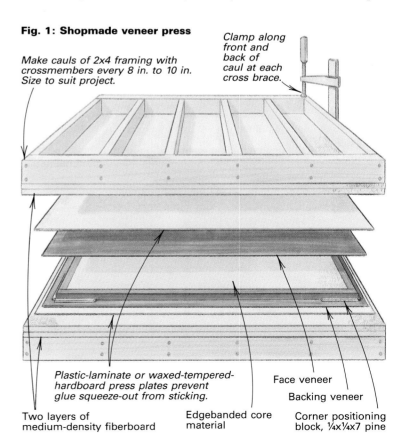

Make cauls of 2x4 framing with crossmembers every 8 in. to 10 in. Size to suit project.

Clamp along front and back of caul at each cross brace.

Plastic-laminate or waxed-tempered-hardboard press plates prevent glue squeeze-out from sticking.

Face veneer

Backing veneer

Two layers of medium-density fiberboard

Edgebanded core material

Corner positioning block, 1/4x1/4x7 pine

Above: The club and spade inlays add an interesting detail to the plain cabinet exterior. The knobs are glued up from endgrain and are edge-veneered to emphasize their shapes. The diamond knob operates the cabinet latch. Left: The inlaid veneer in the drawers will challenge your veneering skills. Custom trays and racks can be designed to accommodate your particular games and storage needs.

strips of one veneer and four strips of a contrasting color. Clamp the veneer strips between two solid pieces of ¾x1¾x18 stock by screwing the solid stock together at the ends, without screwing through the veneer, and then plane the protruding edges of veneer flush to the clamping stock. Remove the clamping stock and tape the veneer strips together, alternating the colors. Then, with a straightedge guide and an X-Acto knife, cut across the alternating strips to form 1¾-in. strips with contrasting colored squares of veneer. Reposition and tape these strips to form the checkerboard pattern by offsetting every other row. The diagonal-stripe edging is made by alternating ½-in. strips of ebony or gray-dyed maple with maple and then crosscutting on an angle instead of straight across the veneer strips as the checkerboard was done. After trimming off the extra squares at either end, laminate the checkerboard to ½-in. particleboard and add the striped edging.

Building the carcase — Begin by determining the size cabinet you want. My cabinet was designed in Germany to fit continental game sizes, but American game boards in general and your collection of games in particular may dictate different dimensions. Work backward from your finished dimensions, subtracting the thickness of veneers and solid edgebandings to find the size of the core panels. Depending on the veneer, I used ¼-in.-thick mahogany or maple edgebanding, mitered at the corners, on all edges of each piece, except on the mating edges of the doors and on the ends of the carcase pieces. Here, ½-in.-thick edgebanding provides extra stock for rabbeting the door edges and mitering the carcase corners. Edgebanding at the ends of the carcase pieces allows me to slightly ease the mitered joint if necessary without fear of sanding through the veneer to the core. I wanted to match the faces of the panels as closely as possible, but was unable to get solid edgebanding stock to match my veneers; so I veneered all the exposed panel edges with mahogany from the same flitch used for the face veneers. Edge veneers are particularly recommended when using aniline- or alcohol-base stains to ensure even color. Before staining, raise the grain with a slightly damp rag and then lightly sand with 180-grit paper to remove the fuzz.

With all of the individual panels veneered, I began the actual construction by rabbeting the back edge of the sides, top and bottom, ½ in. deep by 1 in. wide, to accept the maple-veneered particleboard back and to conceal the French cleat used to hang the cabinet. I drilled the holes for the plastic miter dowels before mitering the ends of the carcase pieces, and then I drilled the holes for the adjustable shelves as well as the holes for the ⅜-in.-dia. by 2-in.-long dowels that join the fixed shelves and vertical dividers. The plastic miter dowels made dry-fitting these parts much easier. Before final assembly, all parts were sanded with 100-grit and then 150-grit paper. Although the back is dry-fitted during construction, it is not glued and screwed into its rabbet until after the carcase is assembled, the drawer guides installed and the interior lacquered. To make the French cleat, rip a ¾x5x31½ maple board down the center with the sawblade at a 30° angle. The top half of the board, glued and screwed to the cabinet back, hooks over the bottom half of the board, screwed to the wall, to hang the cabinet.

Dovetail and fit the solid-maple drawers, shown in the bottom photo above, to their openings before dadoing the drawer-guide slots and rabbeting the sides for the bottom. The ³⁄₁₆-in. maple-veneered plywood bottoms are glued and screwed into the side rabbets and simply butt against the front and back of the drawer. The inlaid front screwed to the drawer is solid mahogany with veneers on both sides. The back of the drawer front is veneered with vertical-grain mahogany. Then, I rout an inset in the face of the drawer front to accommodate a double layer of veneer. A vertical-grain mahogany substrate provides a good base for the maple veneer that

also work well. Veneers like oak, mahogany, teak and basswood are better saved for later projects because they are brittle. If I'm inlaying small straight pieces in a soft veneer, I can just press the background veneer down on top of the inlay veneer and cut through both layers in one pass. To do this, hold the knife at 65° to 70° with your hand tipped to the center of the inlay. The resulting inlay will be slightly larger than the opening, and when inserted from the back, it will eliminate gaps between the inlay and the background veneer. For the more brittle veneers, I first cut out the pattern from the background veneer and then lay the background veneer over the inlay veneer to lightly trace the pattern with my knife. To prevent movement while tracing these inlays, it helps to first cut the inlay piece slightly oversize and tape it to the back of the background piece. After tracing the pattern, remove the background veneer and complete the cut by making several light passes on the inlay veneer. The most difficult veneers to work without damaging are ebony, rosewood, tulip wood and any burl. To avoid splitting and breaking these veneers, I cover the entire back with paper veneering tape and then make numerous light passes to complete the cut. The backing tape must be removed before glue-up.

When making up an inlay of several small pieces, like the joker on the drawer bottom in the photo on p. 60, I use clear tape to hold the cut pieces in place as I go, which allows me to see the design as I work. Once the inlay is complete, I tape it into the background and then hold it up to the light and check for gaps and broken pieces. After the inlay is glued in place, I remove the tape by gently pulling it across the grain to avoid lifting the veneer.

When I'm making the game boards, I use the same technique to prepare the veneer for the field and the edging. To make the checkerboard with 1¾-in. squares for example, first cut veneer strips about 16 in. long and about 2¼ in. wide. You will need five

Fig. 2: Game cabinet

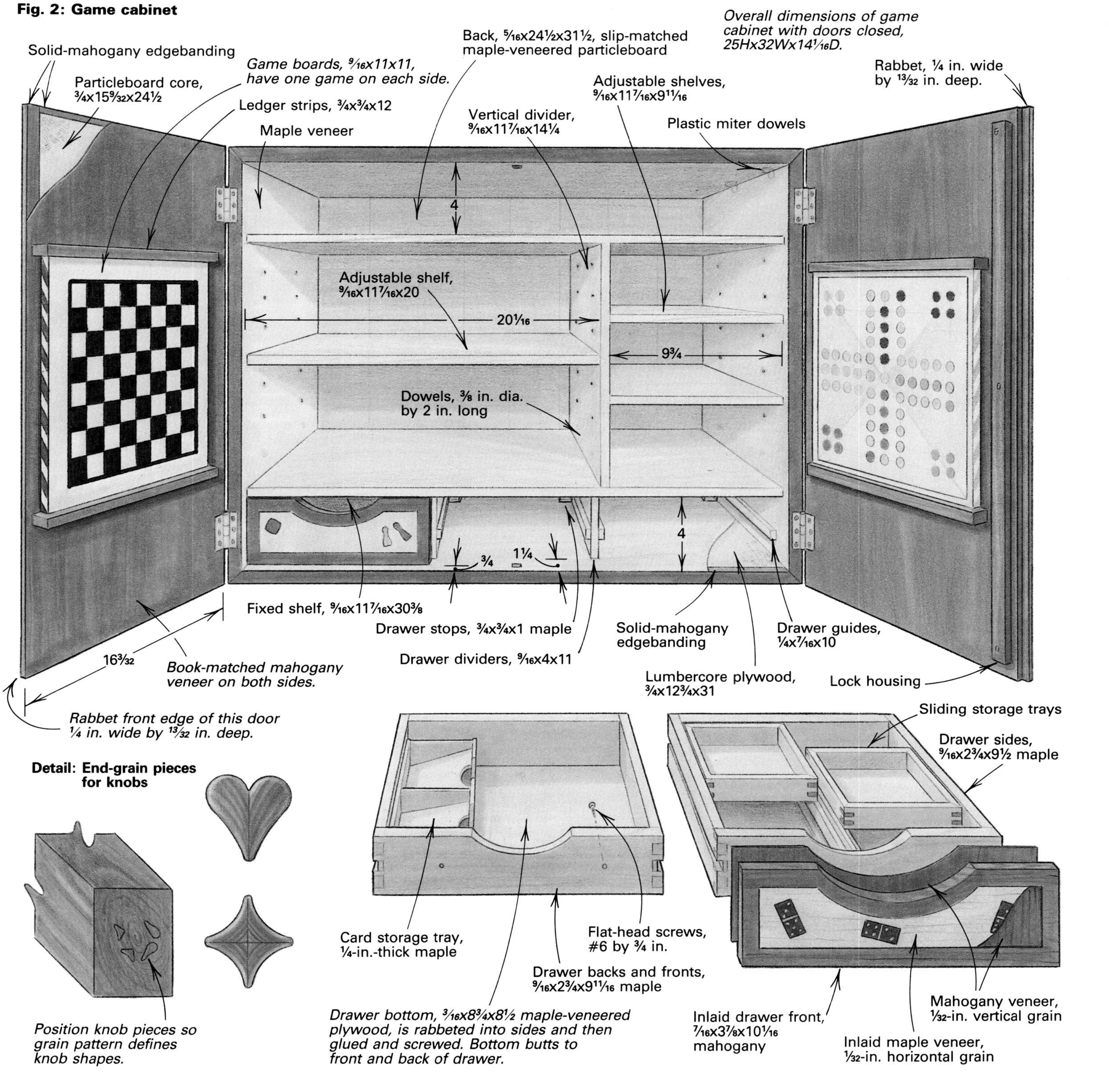

Overall dimensions of game cabinet with doors closed, 25Hx32Wx14¹⁄₁₆D.
Solid-mahogany edgebanding
Particleboard core, ¾x15⁹⁄₃₂x24½
Game boards, ⁹⁄₁₆x11x11, have one game on each side.
Ledger strips, ¾x¾x12
Maple veneer
Back, ⁵⁄₁₆x24½x31½, slip-matched maple-veneered particleboard
Vertical divider, ⁹⁄₁₆x11⁷⁄₁₆x14¼
Adjustable shelves, ⁹⁄₁₆x11⁷⁄₁₆x9¹¹⁄₁₆
Plastic miter dowels
Rabbet, ¼ in. wide by ¹³⁄₃₂ in. deep.
4
Adjustable shelf, ⁹⁄₁₆x11⁷⁄₁₆x20
20¹⁄₁₆
9¾
Dowels, ⅜ in. dia. by 2 in. long
4
¾
1¼
Fixed shelf, ⁹⁄₁₆x11⁷⁄₁₆x30⅜
Drawer stops, ¾x¾x1 maple
Drawer dividers, ⁹⁄₁₆x4x11
Solid-mahogany edgebanding
Drawer guides, ¼x⁷⁄₁₆x10
Lumbercore plywood, ¾x12¾x31
Lock housing
16³⁄₃₂
Book-matched mahogany veneer on both sides.
Rabbet front edge of this door ¼ in. wide by ¹³⁄₃₂ in. deep.
Detail: End-grain pieces for knobs
Position knob pieces so grain pattern defines knob shapes.
Sliding storage trays
Drawer sides, ⁹⁄₁₆x2¾x9½ maple
Card storage tray, ¼-in.-thick maple
Flat-head screws, #6 by ¾ in.
Drawer backs and fronts, ⁹⁄₁₆x2¾x9¹¹⁄₁₆ maple
Drawer bottom, ³⁄₁₆x8¾x8½ maple-veneered plywood, is rabbeted into sides and then glued and screwed. Bottom butts to front and back of drawer.
Inlaid drawer front, ⁷⁄₁₆x3⅞x10¹⁄₁₆ mahogany
Mahogany veneer, ¹⁄₃₂-in. vertical grain
Inlaid maple veneer, ¹⁄₃₂-in. horizontal grain

has grain running in the same direction as the solid drawer front.

The doors are built, as detailed in figure 2, with ½-in.-wide edgebanding on their mating edges. Rabbets cut into this edge form a lap joint so that the right door overlaps the left. This way, the locking mechanism, two sliding bars operated by turning the knob, will also hold the left door closed. I made the doorknobs from sections of endgrain glued together, so the grain pattern reflects the design of the knob, and then chiseled, carved and sanded the knobs to shape. The veneer edging strips were glued on with contact cement because it's difficult to clamp these odd shapes. While contact cement works well in this application, and is the adhesive of choice for plastic-laminate work, I don't recommend it for general veneer work because it has a tendency to soften and loosen over time and it can cause the veneer to shrink, leaving gaps up to ¹⁄₁₆ in. wide. Also, solvents in many finishing products can penetrate the veneer and hasten the softening process. The ledger strips holding the game boards on the back of the doors work just like a sliding-door track. The rabbet in the bottom ledger is ³⁄₁₆ in. deep and the rabbet in the top ledger is ⅜ in. deep so that the top of the board may be raised into the top ledger to move the bottom of the board into or out of the bottom ledger. □

Norbert Heinold builds custom cabinets and veneered pieces in Canoga Park, Cal.

New Tools Make Laminating Easy

Big baggies and vacuum pumps put the squeeze on veneers

by Monroe Robinson

Premium wood veneers can turn a perfectly ordinary woodworking project into a spectacular display of color, pattern and light. It's just too bad that many woodworkers shy away from veneering because veneer presses cost a lot of money and take up a lot of shop space to boot.

But now there is an inexpensive and space-saving solution to veneering, which is almost foolproof in operation, stores easily out of the way and can exert a force of 1,900 pounds per square foot. It's a vacuum press. A giant zip-lock bag with a

vacuum pump attached, this startlingly simple device can replace the old-style mechanical press for veneering, laminating and some bending operations. And curved forms can be veneered without complicated matching molds, as shown in the photo below.

Woodworkers have also discovered that vacuum pumps can hold workpieces safely for routing, drilling and a variety of other operations. There are now at least six companies that offer a variety of vacuum systems. And most of these systems are priced well under $1,000.

How vacuum bagging works

At sea level, atmospheric pressure applies 14.7 pounds per square inch (psi) of force on everything, in all directions. As you draw a vacuum within a bag, you remove the air at equilibrium with the atmospheric pressure, which (measured in inches of mercury) then bears in on the bag from all directions. Thirty inches of mercury (in. Hg.), which is the maximum possible, is equivalent to 14.7-psi pressure at sea level. The systems we use in woodworking are designed to remove up to 90% of the air for a vacuum pressure of 27 in. Hg. (13.23 psi) at sea level.

Types of vacuum pumps

Two different types of pumps are used to draw a vacuum for these presses: an electric-powered rotary-vane vacuum pump and a compressed-air-powered venturi pump. Rotary-vane pumps work like an air compressor in reverse, sucking air from inside the bag. Venturi pumps send compressed air rushing through a restricted orifice, which generates the vacuum. They're lightweight, compact and have no moving parts.

To compare the pumps, I put a curved, 7-cu.-ft., hollow form in a standard-sized 4-ft. by 8-ft. bag. I connected each pump via its own hose to this setup and timed how long it took the pump to reach a vacuum of 23 in. Hg.

All four of the rotary-vane units shown in the top photo on the facing page use the same setup: a 1/4-HP, electric motor and an oil-less rotary-vane vacuum pump rated at five cubic feet per minute (CFM). In spite of this similar setup, their performance ranged from 4 minutes to 11 minutes to draw 23 in. Hg. in the test bag (see the chart on p. 67). The difference can be explained in two words: *flow restriction*. The pumps from Vacuum Pressing Systems and Mercury Vacuum Presses avoid flow restriction by using 3/8-in.-inside diameter (ID) hoses. The poorer performing units

***Because vacuum presses** can easily clamp and form contoured shapes as well as flat panels, they are opening up veneering and bent laminating to the average woodworker. Their reasonable cost, convenience and storability make them appropriate for most shops.*

from Woodworker's Supply and Vacuum Tool Co. have ⅛-in.-ID hoses. More than about six minutes could become a problem, depending on the working time of the adhesive and the complexity of the piece being pressed.

Vacuum Tool Co.'s pump is manually controlled; the other rotary-vane pumps have automatic controls with an adjustable switch for setting the vacuum pressure at which the pump shuts off. On Vacuum Pressing Systems' and Woodworker's Supply's systems, setting the switch is an easy screwdriver adjustment.

These automatic switches have a preset lower level to turn the pump back on when the vacuum drops to the preset point, usually 19 in. to 20 in. Hg. The gap between upper and lower levels is called the dead band. The narrower the dead band, the more often the pump will recycle. A narrow dead band coupled with a leaky bag could cause a pump to cycle on and off every few seconds.

The dead bands for the supplied units ranged from 3 in. to 5 in. Hg. and all worked well except Woodworker's Supply's system. This pump dropped 2 in. to 3 in. Hg. at cutoff, effectively reducing the dead band to only 1 in. to 1½ in. Hg.

While venturi pumps are generally less expensive than rotary-vane pumps, there is the additional cost of an air compressor. Venturi pumps are available in automatic and manual models (see the photos at right). The automatic venturi pumps use an electrically operated solenoid valve to turn the pump on and off at a desired vacuum level. All these pumps have a dead band of about 3 in. Hg., and all their switches are easy to adjust. Each of the automatic switching units worked well.

The venturis' pumping rates ranged between 1 CFM and 4 CFM, and their performances generally fell in the middle of the rotary-vane systems. Unlike rotary-vane pumps, the performance differences of the venturi pumps are almost directly related to their rated capacities (see the chart).

Venturi pumps work best if they have a filter on the vacuum line to remove particles that might plug the venturi and a water-catching filter on the compressed air line. Unless filtered out, water passing from the compressor through the venturi decreases the pump's efficiency. Mercury Vacuum Presses' automatic venturi has a filter on the vacuum line that's easy to see and to clean and a filter on the compressed air line. Vacuum Pressing Systems also filters the vacuum line. If missing, filters can be added easily to either the vacuum or the compressed air lines.

Rotary-vane vacuum pumps, *arranged from left to right according to increasing list price, include units from Vacuum Tool Co., Woodworker's Supply, Vacuum Pressing Systems and Mercury Vacuum Presses. Rotary-vane pumps are the best choice for moderate-to-heavy vacuum pressing requirements. Also shown under each unit are its closure systems and vacuum line connections.*

Automatic venturi pumps *with bags, arranged from left to right by price: Quality VAKuum Products, Vacuum Pressing Systems and Mercury Vacuum Presses. Powered by an air compressor, venturis are generally a little slower than rotary-vane pumps but usually a little cheaper as well and are suitable for light-to-moderate vacuum pressing.*

Manual venturi pumps, *arranged from left to right by price: Gougeon Brothers, Quality VAKuum Products, Vacuum Pressing Systems and Mercury Vacuum Presses. Manual venturi pumps offer a low-cost introduction to the many benefits of using vacuum.*

Vacuum bags and bagging films

Most vacuum bags are made of either vinyl or polyurethane and come in many sizes. I looked at standard-sized bags that could handle a full 4x8 sheet of material. The bag systems require a grid board inside the bag that serves as the bottom platen. The grid board is typically made of ¾-in.-thick medium-density fiberboard (MDF) with ⅛-in.-wide by ⅛-in.-deep grooves cut on 4 in. to 10 in. centers in both directions. The hose from the pump connects to the bag and to a cross in the grid. The grid permits free flow of air throughout the bag. The two systems in this review that employ films rather than bags use a breather fabric in place of the grid board.

A bag could hold a vacuum almost indefinitely were it not for the leaks that develop at the closure, connections, filters, check valves and in the bag itself. To minimize leaks, check and tighten fittings and take proper care of the bags. Regular cleaning of glue and debris and not stressing the seams will prolong a bag's life.

The bagging materials offered by the manufacturers are 2-mil, modified nylon-resin film (from which you can make a bag), 20-mil vinyl, 30-mil vinyl and 20-mil urethane. Of the three types of bags, the 20-mil vinyl bags are the least expensive and most commonly used. Although more prone to punctures and tearing at the seams, they'll last for years under normal use. Vacuum Pressing Systems' 20-mil bag comes with a clear top and a solid-blue 30-mil bottom.

The tougher 30-mil vinyl bag is recommended for medium-to-heavy use. It's also stiffer, which I found made it easier to load the bag.

Vacuum Pressing Systems also sells a 20-mil polyurethane bag. The urethane film is much tougher and harder to puncture than either the 20-mil or 30-mil vinyl bags and will stand up to the heaviest commercial use.

A couple of manufacturers supply a thin 2-mil, modified nylon-resin film designed for one-time use. It is usually used as a single top film and taped to an impervious surface. Taping around the edges takes a while, and it is difficult to get a good seal. For this reason, these manufacturers offer continuous running pumps.

Hose connections to the bags varied in location and convenience. Depending on the manufacturer, the hose might connect at the top, side or bottom of the bag. I found the quick-disconnect coupling on Vacuum Pressing Systems' bags to be the most convenient. To attach a hose to the nylon film, both Gougeon Brothers and Vacuum Tool Co. sell a bag tap fitting. I preferred the one from Vacuum Tool Co. because it has two parts that screw together from each side of the film.

Closure systems

I used the interval between pump cycles as a measure of bag and closure integrity. Because all the bags were new with no leaks, the recycle interval primarily revealed the effectiveness of the closures.

Each manufacturer uses a different closure system. Woodworker's Supply uses a light-weight zipper that is fast and easy, but it didn't seal the bag very well, even with the recommended sealing tape at the ends of the zipper. Its recycle interval averaged about 30 minutes.

Mercury Vacuum Presses also uses a zipper, but it's heavy-duty and requires pushing your finger along its length to get the best seal. Although recycle times varied, this system could hold a vacuum for up to two hours. Mercury also offers bags with zippers at both ends or custom bags to meet special needs, such as a zipper along three sides for easy loading and a narrow bag with a 30-ft.-long zipper for pressing spiral staircase parts.

Vacuum Pressing Systems' bags have neat little hook-and-loop fastner tabs to hold the bag temporarily around a ¾-in.-dia. plastic rod, making it easy to snap an extruded plastic C-channel around the rod and bag. This closure is simple to apply and provides the most effective seal, holding a vacuum for well over six hours before the pump recycled. Closures at both ends of Vacuum Pressing Systems' large bags allow easy loading of multiple pieces. The seams on Vacuum Pressing Systems' bags are small and smoothly welded to-

Shopmade vacuum press for under $100

by Larry Schiffer

I was faced with the prospect of veneering a kitchen full of cabinets for my son's new log home and had decided a vacuum press was the way to go. My problem was finding a source for the vinyl in less than 5,000-sq.-ft. rolls. I was stymied until one day while shopping at K-Mart, I saw a roll of 5-mil.-thick vinyl for storm windows that only costs $10. I decided to experiment.

Making the bag: I folded the vinyl in half to make a 54-in. by 72-in. bag and welded the edges with some PVC solvent from my local home-building center. I installed a pump-connection fitting, as shown in the sketch, using ⅛-in.-ID all-thread pipe. I further reinforced this critical juncture with a generous application of pool patch, available from most pool-supply outlets. Pool patch is a highly viscous vinyl cementing material, which allows a greater buildup of material and a stronger joint. To help protect the thin vinyl, I rounded all edges of the MDF platen. Some ⅜-in.-ID vinyl tubing connects the bag to the pump (see the photo at left).

Connecting the pump: For a pump, I used a single-cylinder air compressor. I removed the air filter and, using a compression fitting, attached a piece of ⅜-in. copper tubing to the suction side of the air compressor. The vinyl hose from the bag slips over the copper tubing. The air from the pressure side outlet of the compressor discharges into the room. To protect the compressor's motor, I loosened the belt tension so that when I hear the compressor start to lug, the belt slips. Although using an air compressor in this manner invites the discharge of small amounts of oil from the crankcase, I haven't had to add any oil in two years of operation. As an alternative to the air compressor, you can get a surplus or used vacuum pump from the Surplus Center (1015 West O St., Lincoln, Neb. 68501; 800-488-3407). □

Larry Schiffer is a woodworker in Hopewell Junction, N.Y.

Vacuum line to bag connection

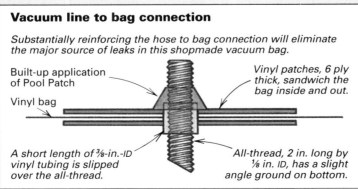

Substantially reinforcing the hose to bag connection will eliminate the major source of leaks in this shopmade vacuum bag.

Built-up application of Pool Patch

Vinyl bag

Vinyl patches, 6 ply thick, sandwich the bag inside and out.

A short length of ⅜-in.-ID vinyl tubing is slipped over the all-thread.

All-thread, 2 in. long by ⅛ in. ID, has a slight angle ground on bottom.

gether to create a tight-sealing bag.

Quality VAKuum Products gives instructions to make a rod closure that is not as convenient as Vacuum Pressing Systems' but is equally effective—holding a vacuum for more than six hours.

Conclusions

The best pump and bag combination will depend on your use and the equipment you currently own. Manual venturi pumps are the least expensive, provided you already own an air compressor. With this setup, you're faced with the option of letting the compressor run continuously or with the inconvenience of monitoring the system. By adding a vacuum-storage tank, you can increase the volume of the system and extend the recycle time. Quality VAKuum Products sells components, so you can start with a manual venturi and add an automatic control kit later. One drawback of the manual venturi pumps, except Vacuum Pressing Systems' pump, is that they generate more than 85 decibels of noise, a level I wouldn't want to listen to for long.

If I had a compressor and intended to do only a modest amount of vacuum pumping, I would probably get an automatic venturi system. The higher volume automatic venturis performed almost as well as the better rotary-vane pumps. And a venturi pump is the better choice for hold-down applications.

Because I do a lot of veneer work, I prefer the top-end automatic, rotary-vane systems. In a production situation, these pumps are cheaper to operate than the compressor-powered venturis. And their ability to quickly draw a vacuum can be critical when working with complicated glue-ups that take longer to assemble and get in the bag.

The right bag material will depend on how frequently you will use the bag, as previously discussed. Because the zipper closure is flexible and will wrap around the workpiece, you can press larger forms with this type of bag. But I prefer the tight seal and convenience of Vacuum Pressing Systems' rod closure. The 2-mil, modified resin film might be a good choice for unusual applications because it's cheap, it can be taped together to make a bag of any size and it will conform to any shape.

Manufacturer's instructions vary from none (Vacuum Tool Co.) to a complete book, *Advanced Vacuum Bagging Techniques*, from Gougeon Brothers, which deals primarily in epoxy techniques. In between are Woodworker's Supply (two pages) and Quality VAKuum Products (four pages), which cover the basics. Both Vacuum Pressing Systems and Mercury Vacuum Presses provide manuals that go well beyond the basics and include information on techniques and adhesives.

Vacuum pressing is an emerging technology that is making the process of pressing and laminating veneers available to almost any woodworker. Improvements and refinements in pumps, bags and closure systems were under development by several manufacturers while this article was being prepared. These new systems weren't ready in time for review, so check for current developments before you buy any system. □

Monroe Robinson is a woodworker in Little River, Calif.

Vacuum Press Systems

| Manufacturer | Pumps | | | | Bags | | |
	Type	Vacuum flow in CFM	Time to evacuate bag (min:sec) ▶	List ● price	Bag or film material	Closure system	List ● price
Gougeon Brothers, Inc. PO Box 908 Bay City, MI 48707 (517) 684-7286	Manual venturi	1.0	15:0 ✳	$65	2-mil film (60 in. wide)	Tape	$30
Mercury Vacuum Presses PO Box 2232 Fort Bragg, CA 95437 (800) 995-4506	Auto. rotary vane Auto. venturi Manual venturi	5 4 4	4:40 6:15 6:20	$640 $438 $189	20-mil vinyl 30-mil vinyl	Heavy zipper	$129 $165
Quality VAKuum Products Inc. 32 Longmeadow Road Lincoln, MA 01773 (800) 547-5484	Auto. venturi Manual venturi	3.2 1.6	6:05 10:0	$320 $99	20-mil vinyl	None	$155
Vacuum Pressing Systems, Inc. 553 River Road Brunswick, ME 04011 (207) 725-0935	Auto. rotary vane Auto. venturi Manual venturi	5 3.2 2	4:10 6:45 8:35	$605 $430 $139	20-mil vinyl 30-mil vinyl 20-mil urethane	Rod and C-channel	$135 $178 $420
Vacuum Tool Co. 310 Watertown Road Morris, CT 06763 (203) 567-3499	Manual rotary vane	5	11:20	$425	2-mil film (72 in. x 30 yds.)	Tape	$74
Woodworker's Supply, Inc. 1108 N. Glenn Road Casper, WY 82601 (800) 645-9292	Auto. rotary vane	5	9:40	$449	20-mil vinyl	Light zipper	$109 ▲

✳ Pump requires 15 min. to draw a maximum of 18 in. Hg.
▶ The time required to draw 23 in. Hg. in a 4x8 bag containing a 7-cu.-ft. hollow form.

● To determine system prices, add the selected bag price to the selected pump price.
▲ Woodworker's Supply offers a complete-system price of $529.

An Oval Semainier

Quick-set veneering a bendable-plywood carcase

by Reid H. Leonard, Ph.D.

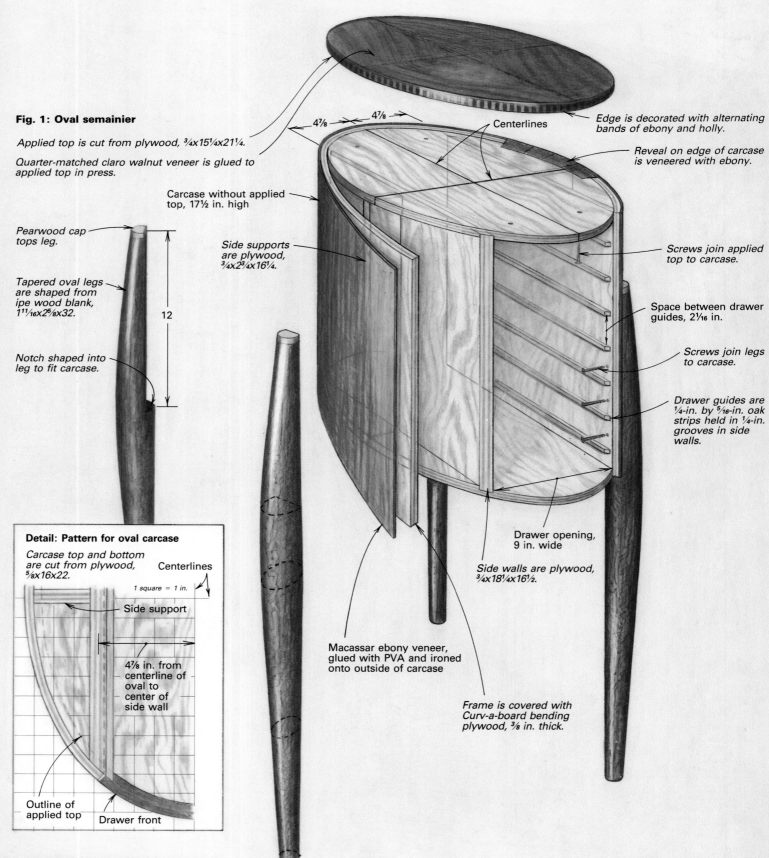

Fig. 1: Oval semainier

Applied top is cut from plywood, ³⁄₄x15¹⁄₄x21¹⁄₄.

Quarter-matched claro walnut veneer is glued to applied top in press.

Centerlines

Edge is decorated with alternating bands of ebony and holly.

Reveal on edge of carcase is veneered with ebony.

4⁷⁄₈   4⁷⁄₈

Carcase without applied top, 17½ in. high

Pearwood cap tops leg.

Tapered oval legs are shaped from ipe wood blank, 1¹¹⁄₁₆x2⁵⁄₈x32.

12

Notch shaped into leg to fit carcase.

Side supports are plywood, ³⁄₄x2³⁄₄x16¹⁄₄.

Screws join applied top to carcase.

Space between drawer guides, 2¹⁄₁₆ in.

Screws join legs to carcase.

Drawer guides are ¼-in. by ⁵⁄₁₆-in. oak strips held in ¼-in. grooves in side walls.

Drawer opening, 9 in. wide

Side walls are plywood, ³⁄₄x18¹⁄₄x16½.

Macassar ebony veneer, glued with PVA and ironed onto outside of carcase

Frame is covered with Curv-a-board bending plywood, ³⁄₈ in. thick.

Detail: Pattern for oval carcase

Carcase top and bottom are cut from plywood, ⁵⁄₈x16x22.

Centerlines

1 square = 1 in.

Side support

4⁷⁄₈ in. from centerline of oval to center of side wall

Outline of applied top

Drawer front

Photos: Sandor Nagyszalanczy; drawings: Lee Hov

I've been participating in arts and crafts shows for years, displaying a wide range of woodwork including tall, seven-drawer cabinets the French call "semainiers." In the last two decades I've made more than 35 semainiers in sizes suitable as sculpture stands or flat files or for lingerie, jewelry or silverware. I built most of these from a secondary wood or plywood and covered it with veneers from my eclectic collection of exotic and domestic species. Veneer lets me use rare woods in an economical way, and it allows decorative patterns not possible with solid lumber.

Although I've also built round and square semainiers, my favorite, shown in the photo below, is oval. But because oval-shaped cabinets, such as those often employed in Parisian Art Deco designs, are difficult to build by standard coopering—not to mention difficult to veneer—I've developed my own method for oval carcases. It involves wrapping a simple plywood frame with a special bending plywood, and then veneering it using white glue (polyvinyl acetate) as an adhesive, pressed and quick-set into place with a regular household iron. In this article I'll tell you in detail how I built my oval semainier, starting with a plywood carcase.

Building the carcase—The carcase consists of a basic plywood frame covered with the bending plywood. The top and bottom of the case were made first, starting with two pieces of ⅝-in. plywood, each 16 in. wide by 22 in. long. After drawing centerlines down the length, width and edges of each piece, I plowed a pair of ¾-in.-wide by ⅛-in.-deep grooves with a dado blade on my tablesaw. Each pair of grooves was centered 4⅞ in. to either side of the lengthwise centerline (see figure 1). These grooves accept the vertical side walls that connect the top and bottom and form a 9-in.-wide drawer compartment. After plowing the grooves, I drew a 16-in. by 22-in. oval on only the top blank, tacked it to the bottom blank with small brads, and cut out both ovals at once with a sabersaw. With the two ovals still tacked together, I sanded their edges smooth, and then separated them and pulled out the brads. I also cut out the cabinet's two ¾-in. plywood side supports at this time, each 2¾ in. wide by 16¼ in. long.

Next, I cut the two side walls, each 16½ in. wide by 18¼ in. long, from ¾-in. plywood. The drawer-facing surface of each side must receive seven grooves, cut with a dado blade, to house the drawer-guide strips. The grooves are laid out on only one side wall, spaced as shown in figure 1. Since all the drawers are the same depth, this layout work is critical and should be done with a marking knife. Following the marks, I set my tablesaw's rip fence for the first ¼-in.-wide by ⅛-in.-deep groove and then dadoed both side walls. I repeated this process until all the grooves were done.

The 14 oak drawer-guide strips were ripped on the tablesaw to their ¼x⁵⁄₁₆x18 final dimensions. They were then glued and clamped into their grooves in the side walls. Make sure the guides are well seated in their grooves. Having been careless at times myself, I know from experience that a high-riding drawer-guide strip can create all kinds of trouble later when you're fitting the drawers.

Next I assembled the plywood frame pieces, first applying glue into the dadoes in the top and bottom, and then setting the side walls and side support strips in place. The assembly can be clamped, nailed or stapled until the glue sets. It's important to keep the drawer compartment square during glue-up, and so I cut two scrap pieces and temporarily tacked them across the ends of the sides. After the glue was well set, I handplaned the square edges of the side walls that projected slightly beyond the top and bottom, and then smoothed them to conform to the oval.

Applying the covering—To create a continuous surface on the outside of my semainier, I used Curv-a-board bending plywood

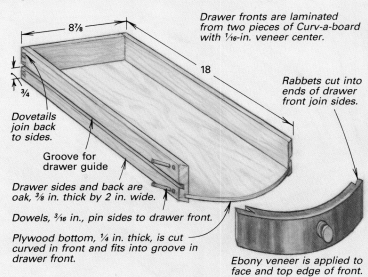

Fig. 2: Curved-front drawer

Drawer fronts are laminated from two pieces of Curv-a-board with ¹⁄₁₆-in. veneer center.

Rabbets cut into ends of drawer front join sides.

Dovetails join back to sides.

Groove for drawer guide

Drawer sides and back are oak, ⅜ in. thick by 2 in. wide.

Dowels, ³⁄₁₆ in., pin sides to drawer front.

Plywood bottom, ¼ in. thick, is cut curved in front and fits into groove in drawer front.

Ebony veneer is applied to face and top edge of front.

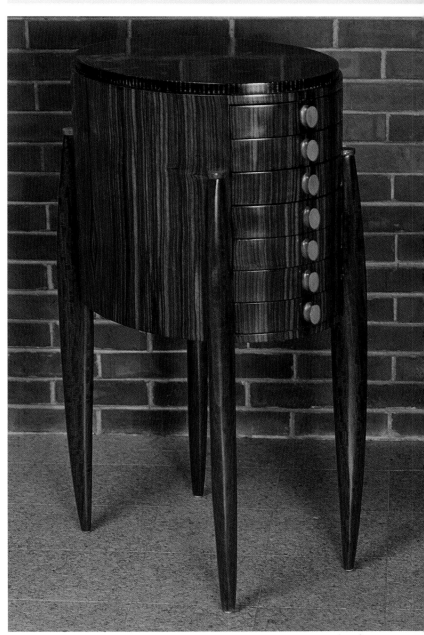

Leonard built this seven-drawer cabinet, called a semainier by the French, from ebony-veneered plywood, using his own method of constructing and veneering a curved carcase.

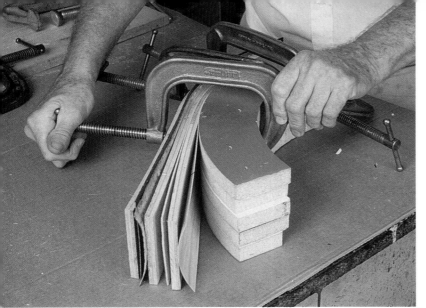

After making a caul from scraps of particleboard, the author clamps up one of the curved drawer fronts to form a sandwich of bending plywood around a veneer center. Scraps of bending ply and veneer cushion the front while it's being clamped.

Leonard employs an unusual method to apply the veneer to the outside of his semainier: PVA glue that he quick-sets by heating the veneer with a clothes iron. Here, he tests the iron's heat on a scrap to make sure it won't scorch the veneer.

from Paxton Lumber Co., 1815 S. Agnew, Oklahoma City, Okla. 73108. Curv-a-board is a 9mm-thick (a little less than ⅜ in.) three-ply board with two lauan outer layers glued over a thin, flexible center ply. Curv-a-board comes in 4-ft. by 8-ft. sheets and bends parallel to the grain, which runs the width of the sheet. For my first trial with this material, I covered a 12-in.-dia. cylinder, and it worked very well.

I covered the exterior of the oval semainier frame by wrapping it with a single sheet of 17¾-in.-wide by 53-in.-long Curv-a-board. I started by tacking one edge of the ply to the front left side wall, wrapping the ply around the back, and gluing and nailing it down with 3d box nails as I worked around the case. I like nails because their heads hold the soft lauan while the glue sets. The Curv-a-board moaned in protest while it was bent, but it didn't break. Once the sheet was tacked to the right side wall, I used a sabersaw and rasp to trim the ends flush to the drawer opening. I also belt-sanded the slight overhang on the top and bottom of the case. Next, two narrow strips of Curv-a-board were glued and nailed to the edge of the top and bottom around the drawer opening. The nail heads were set below the surface and the seams between these strips and the main panel were sanded flush. I then filled the holes, as well as any other defects, seams or cracks, with auto-body putty.

Curved drawers—The drawers for the semainier are basic in their construction (see figure 2 on the previous page), except for their curved fronts, which I laminated to match the contour of the car-

case. Each drawer front was glued up from two layers of Curv-a-board, with a ¹⁄₁₆-in. veneer crossbanding sandwiched in the center, resulting in a final thickness of about ¹³⁄₁₆ in. To make a caul for the lamination process, I started by gluing up a 3-in.-thick blank from some particleboard scraps. With a pencil, I first marked a centerline onto the blank and then drew the curve by tracing the narrow end of the carcase. This curved line represents the shape of the final outside surface of the drawer front. To get the final caul profile, I followed the curved line, marking another line parallel to and ¹³⁄₁₆ in. (the thickness of the drawer front) *inside* of it. Then I bandsawed to this line, smoothed the surface of the caul and re-marked the centerline.

In preparation for gluing up the drawer fronts, I cut enough Curv-a-board and ¹⁄₁₆-in. veneer for seven fronts. I made each front slightly oversize—2⅜ in. wide by 11 in. long—to be trimmed later. After spreading yellow glue between each layer, I clamped the three-layer sandwich in the caul, using scraps of veneer on the inside and Curv-a-board on the outside, to prevent the clamps from denting the surface (see the top photo). After about three hours of clamp time, each laminated front was removed, but first the centerline was transferred to each new drawer front, to serve as an aid in centering and trimming later. The top and bottom edges of each front were then cleaned up with a handplane, until each was 2¼ in. wide.

Next I cut the drawer sides and backs from ⅜-in.-thick oak. The sides are 2 in. wide by 18 in. long and the backs are 2 in. wide by 9 in. long. The drawer backs are through-dovetailed to the sides, which leaves a 8⅞-in.-wide drawer after trimming. After using a dado blade on the tablesaw to plow a groove in the sides and backs for the ¼-in. plywood drawer bottoms, I plowed another set of grooves in the sides for the drawer guides, making them slightly wider than the ¼-in.-wide guide strips. The bottom of this groove was spaced ¾ in. up from the bottom edge of each drawer side.

To join the drawer fronts to the sides, I cut ⅜-in.-wide and about ½-in.-deep rabbets on the ends of each front. I did this again with the dado blade in the tablesaw, using the saw's miter gauge to guide the crosscuts. A groove for the drawer bottom was cut in each front with a kerf-cutting (also called slot-cutting) bit chucked in the router. Finally, I used the inside edge of a drawer front to mark one end of each bottom and then bandsawed each to shape.

With all the drawer parts ready, I assembled the back and sides around the bottom, applying yellow glue to all joints. To pin the sides to the drawer fronts, I drilled two ³⁄₁₆-in. holes through each drawer side and then inserted short dowels. After the glue dried, I tried each drawer with the carcase. Aligning each drawer's center-line with the case, I marked the ends of the drawer fronts and then trimmed them with a belt sander held upside down in my bench vise until they fit the openings. After a little more sanding and checking for unfilled holes or defects, the carcase and drawer fronts were ready to veneer.

Veneering the carcase—I decided to cover the plywood exterior of my oval semainier with veneer from a beautiful flitch of Macassar ebony. First I cut enough leaves of the veneer into 18-in. lengths to cover the approximately 6-ft. circumference of the cabinet when laid out side to side. Then I spread the leaves out on the bench to check the grain pattern, carefully preserving the order in which they came off the flitch. I numbered the consecutive leaves with chalk, and then trimmed their long edges straight and parallel with a straightedge and a veneer saw. The leaves for the drawer fronts were taped together into a mat and set aside, to be applied later.

In lieu of using hot hide glue to attach the veneer or a cumber-some caul for gluing and clamping the veneer, which are the most traditional methods, I've developed a procedure that works just as well, but requires less skill and preparation to execute. I applied the veneer a leaf at a time using PVA glue as the adhesive. But instead of clamping the veneer down while the glue set, I used a household clothes iron to set the glue quickly. I used Parabond M447 glue (available from Para Chem, Box 127, Simpsonville, S.C. 29681; 803-967-7691) for this method, which I've found dries firmly, doesn't get rubbery and cleans off with sanding better than other PVA glues I've tried.

To apply the veneer, I first brushed on a fairly heavy coat of glue, applying it to the plywood carcase—not the veneer. The veneer leaf was then laid down and temporarily held in position with several small pieces of masking tape at its leading edge. The leaf was then pressed down with the iron set on low heat (350°F to 400°F). I always test a small piece before beginning, shown in the bottom photo on the facing page, to make sure the iron won't scorch the veneer. I moved the iron slowly back and forth over the leaf (not too slowly, or scorching will occur) and followed it with a veneer roller held in my other hand. The method works because the heat evaporates the water in the glue and the roller applies enough pressure on the plasticized glue to keep the veneer flat as the glue dries.

Once the first leaf was in place, each successive leaf was butted up to the last, attached with tape tabs and ironed on as before, with the area near the seam ironed first. You must be constantly watchful for areas where the veneer has lifted; if heat is applied too quickly, the veneer may be lifted by steam. In fact, I have not been able to use this method to veneer large, flat surfaces because the iron remains in full contact with the wood, which overheats the surface and scorches or shrinks the veneer enough to create open seams. On the convex surfaces of the oval carcase, the iron contacted only a narrow area at one time, so overheating wasn't a problem.

After the veneer was applied all the way around, the excess overhanging the top and bottom was carefully trimmed off with a knife (you can also use a laminate trimmer) and the edges were lightly sanded. An oval panel cut from ¾-in. plywood, later screwed to the top of the carcase, serves as the semainier's actual top. This applied top was cut slightly smaller than the case itself; I drew the same oval as before, but this time on a 15¼-in. by 21¼-in. piece. The size difference created a ⅜-in. ledge (also called a reveal) around the top of the finished semainier.

The applied top was veneered next, using four quarter-matched leaves of claro walnut glued with urea formaldehyde and secured in a press until the adhesive cured. The edge of the applied top was then decorated with alternating bands of ⅛-in.-wide holly and ¼-in.-wide ebony veneer. The ⅜-in.-wide reveal around the top of the carcase that's left exposed after the applied top is screwed on must also be veneered; for this job I used ebony veneer scraps, 2 in. or 3 in. wide, orienting the grain radially around the edge.

To veneer the drawer fronts, I used a veneer saw to crosscut the mat, taped together earlier, into seven strips. These strips were then glued on using the PVA-hot iron method described above. I also glued scraps of ebony veneer to the top edge of each front, to hide the laminations. Finally, strips cut from the top and bottom of the mat were ironed onto the edges of the carcase just above and below the drawers.

The legs—All that remained to complete my semainier was to make and install the legs and the drawer pulls. I chose an exotic wood called lapacho (commonly called ipe) for the legs; I had managed to select a piece that had a nicely mottled grain pattern and was a good color match to the ebony veneer on the carcase. Starting with four 1¹¹⁄₁₆x2⅝x32 billets, I bandsawed and hand-shaped them to an oval cross section that tapered at both ends. Ipe

After lacquering the carcase, drawers, drawer pulls, legs and applied top separately, Leonard uses wood screws to join the parts together and complete his oval semainier.

does not shave well with a drawknife or spokeshave—my usual method of shaping such parts. Instead, I used a rasp and coarse sandpaper to do the shaping work. I then cut and shaped a slightly concave notch 12 in. down from the top of the leg where it joins the case, and then drilled pilot holes in the carcase for the screws to attach it. To lend detail, I made four small caps from pearwood and glued them atop the legs. I also chose pearwood for the drawer pulls. I sawed out seven ¾x⅞x1½ oval blanks on the scroll saw and shaped them with a rasp and files. I found it easier to finish the pulls before attaching them to the drawer fronts.

Next, the carcase, drawers and other parts were finish-sanded to 180-grit and then sprayed with sanding sealer. After the sealer had dried, I resanded using 220-grit paper, and then topcoated the parts with four applications of lacquer. The applied top was then wet-sanded with 400-grit paper and sprayed with gloss lacquer, to give it a lustrous finish. After the finish had dried, I took a good look at the cabinet and decided that the color of the walnut was too light in relation to the ebony. Therefore, I resprayed the top with a black toning lacquer, darkening both the top and the holly-ebony band around it. I then sanded through the stain somewhat, which gave the walnut a sort of tortoiseshell appearance; this was a good match for the ebony. All that was left was to screw the legs and applied top to the carcase, and the pulls to the drawer fronts, and then figure out what to fill those seven drawers with. □

Reid Leonard is a woodworker in Pensacola, Fla.

Marquetry Step by Step

Double-bevel cutting makes the process easy and accurate

by Gregg Zall

Flawless marquetry may be easier than you think. *The marquetry detailing across the drawers on the author's cabinet uses the natural colors of wood to paint a picture. The technique he uses ensures that pieces fit together correctly.*

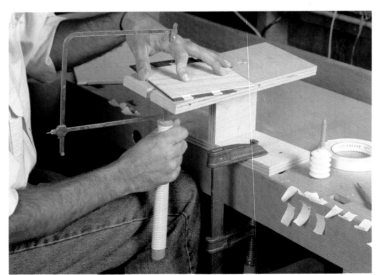

Tilt the table, not the saw. *A plywood cutting table tilted at 8° creates the beveled edges of inlay and background pieces. The author moves a jeweler's saw straight up and down, not at an angle, and pulls the work into the saw to cut the patterns.*

At woodworking school, I was given the time and the confidence to stretch my cabinetmaking skills to the limit. I challenged myself to include graphic arts in my cabinets, which would combine my love of drawing and furnituremaking. Painting surfaces seemed a shame, though, because paint covers up the wood. Instead, I decided to use the natural colors of wood to create pictures with marquetry.

After a lot of trial, error and advice, I came across a method called double-bevel cutting, which gave me the small, accurate details that I wanted on my cabinets, like the birds across the drawer fronts in the cabinet shown above. There are no distracting gluelines in the finished piece.

How is it done? First tape two pieces of veneer together like a sandwich, and then cut out your design, as shown in the photo at left. The trick is that you cut the hole for the inlay and the inlay piece itself simultaneously, so any deviation in the cut is mirrored in both the inlay and the hole.

Because the cut is made at an angle, the inlay piece on the bottom of the sandwich comes out fractionally bigger, taking up the sawkerf and making a perfect fit when glued in, as shown in figure 1 on the facing page. The bevel-edged inlay piece snugs down into the bevel-edged cutout just like the underside of a flathead screw fits into a countersink. It's really not that hard to do. So if you're game, I'll walk you through it step by step.

Photos: Jonathan Binzen

No need to buy veneer. By cutting his own veneer, the author controls the figure of the wood used in the inlays and uses scrap that otherwise might be thrown out. He runs one face of a board over the jointer before cutting the 1/16-in.-thick veneers on a bandsaw.

A palette of natural woods

Natural wood colors, not stain or dye, offer plenty of variety for eye-catching marquetry.

Darks	Reds	Greens
Ebony	Bloodwood	Olive
Walnut	Pernambuco	Lignum vitae
Wenge	Pear	Greenheart
Imbuia	Bubinga	Tulip poplar

Lights	Yellows	Browns
Pear	Osage orange	Fir
Holly	Satinwood	Lacewood
Maple	Boxwood	Mahogany
Madrone	Lignum vitae	Yew
	Nutmeg	Walnut

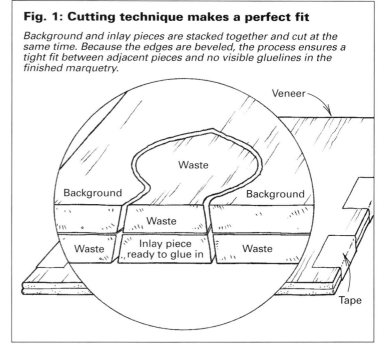

Fig. 1: Cutting technique makes a perfect fit

Background and inlay pieces are stacked together and cut at the same time. Because the edges are beveled, the process ensures a tight fit between adjacent pieces and no visible gluelines in the finished marquetry.

Veneer

Waste

Background

Background

Waste

Waste

Inlay piece ready to glue in

Waste

Tape

Sawing your own veneer

I use my own hand-cut veneers for marquetry. One advantage is that I can pick the wood and figure. All the odd scraps of wood I couldn't bear to toss out are suddenly usable. I have my own favorites, which I've listed by color group in the chart above. Another advantage of cutting my own veneer is that the extra thickness makes the glue joints, and thus the work itself, stronger. I use a bandsaw equipped with a high fence to cut my veneers 1/16 in. thick, as shown in the photo above.

I joint one face of the stock before sawing and then use the veneer just as it comes off the saw. The veneers need to be pretty consistent. Because every bandsaw blade cuts at a slightly different angle, it's essential to clamp a fence to the bandsaw table parallel to the natural drift of the blade. (For more on how to cut your own veneers on the bandsaw, see the article on pp. 20-25.)

Setting up a saw and angled table

If you want to try this marquetry technique and you don't have a scroll saw, try a jeweler's saw with an 8-in.-deep throat (available from Frei and Borel, 126 2nd St., Oakland, Calif. 94607; 800-772-3456). A saw this size allows you to do a 6-in.-sq. design, and this saw is more than capable of producing beautiful work. I fitted mine with a longer handle, like the ones found on Japanese saws. And you'd better buy a few dozen blades because they break often.

There's a little trick to installing blades in a jeweler's saw. First insert one end of the blade in the collet by the handle. The teeth should point down toward the handle. Adjust the saw's frame length so that the top collet is 1/8 in. beyond the end of the blade. Then butt the top end of the saw against the workbench, and flex the frame until the blade fits in the collet. If it's tight enough, it should make a musical note when you pluck it.

A scroll saw would be the next logical step in choosing a tool for marquetry. I use a 20-in. electric scroll saw, which gives me more accuracy and allows me to do bigger designs. For blades, whether you choose a jeweler's saw or a scroll saw, use size 2/0 (2/0, *not* 2).

An angled table is the key to double-bevel cutting. If I'm cutting 1/16-in.-thick veneer on a scroll saw, I tilt the table 8°, but the angle might have to be adjusted for veneers of different thickness. If you're using a jeweler's saw, you'll need to make a simple angled table, as shown in figure 2 on p. 74. I made mine from 3/4-in. plywood and tilted the top at 8°. I cut a notch, or bird's mouth, in the front edge of the table, as figure 2 shows, so the work is supported all around the sawblade. I clamp the table to my bench when I need it and stow it underneath when I don't.

When you're using the jeweler's saw, move the work into the blade, just as you would with a scroll saw. The table holds the work at the correct angle, so keep the saw vertical. You'll probably find it relatively easy to keep the blade from tilting left or right,

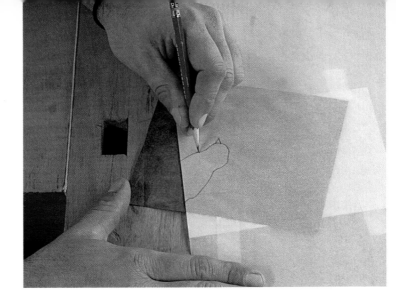

Carbon paper for the design. To transfer patterns to the workpiece, the author starts with tracing paper and then uses carbon paper to reproduce the pattern on the veneer he intends to cut.

Fig. 2: Build the cutting table at an angle

When cutting the beveled pieces by hand, results are more accurate when the saw is held straight and the workpieces are at an angle. The author uses a plywood cutting table with a canted top. For veneers 1/16 in. thick, try an 8° angle, and then add shims to the base of the table to adjust the fit of the background and inlay pieces.

5 in.

8° angle

14 in.

Notch

About 6 in.

Shim here if too loose.

Clamp

Shim here if too tight.

A drill can help get a cut started. When an inlay must be dropped into the middle of a piece, the author starts the cut with a tiny drill bit.

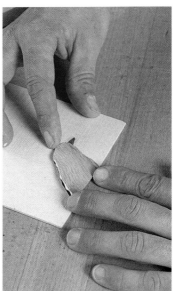

No tape and no clamps. After pieces have been cut out, the author glues the inlay into the background material from the back side.

but you might have to fight the tendency to let the handle of the saw tilt toward you. If your curves consistently come out looking sloppy, this is probably the cause. Make your saw a consistent, smooth, slow-cutting machine that stays in one place at one angle. If your inlay pieces are consistently too tight or too loose, try changing the tilt angle of your table. With the jeweler's saw table, a shim will do the trick. With either the handsaw or scroll saw, keep an eye on any small pieces of veneer. It's easy to lose them.

Start with a simple design

It's time to do some marquetry. First choose a background veneer and a contrasting veneer to inlay into the background. Make a sandwich of the two pieces with the background veneer on top. Tape the veneers together with masking tape. Tape them securely, creasing the tape into the corners with your fingernail. Any movement will distort the final fit of the inlay, so don't reuse the tape.

Draw a design on your background veneer. Except for the simplest designs, I use tracing paper to copy the original. Then I lay the tracing on the veneer with a sheet of carbon or graphite paper between the two and retrace the design, as shown in the top photo.

For a start, try something easy like a little blob. I always cut counterclockwise. Because the teeth on the scroll saw face me as I'm

cutting, tilting the table down from right to left produces the correct bevel. With the jeweler's saw, the teeth face away from me, so I built the table with the opposite tilt—running downward from left to right.

When you feel more confident, try cutting multi-curved blobs and other simple patterns. Now try a point. At the tip of the point, keep your saw moving gently in one spot as you bring the work all the way around. You'll be grinding a small hole, but with practice, the parts will fit correctly.

I need a bunch of clamps, right?

Gluing in the inlay pieces requires no tape and no clamping. Just place the background veneer face down on any flat surface, spread glue on the edges of the inlay piece and press it in from the back (see the bottom right photo). The bevel-to-bevel fit provides the only pressure you need. By the time you get the next piece of inlay veneer taped to the background, the glue will have set enough to let you proceed with the sawing.

Overlay and piercing

Marquetry comes alive when one piece is inlaid over another. This is overlay. You can learn the basics of overlay by cutting a bird's

From *Fine Woodworking* (May 1995) 112:80-83

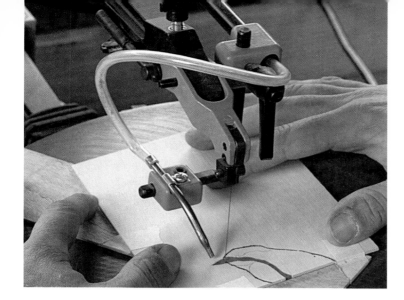

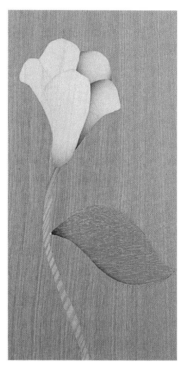

First the beak, then the head. Crisp boundaries are achieved by overlaying one part of a pattern into another, as the author is doing with this bird's beak and head. The scroll-saw table is tilted at 8°.

Hot sand for subtle shading. The finished flower at right gets a sense of visual depth from the shading between adjacent petals. To achieve the effect, the author uses hot sand to scorch the edges of some of the pieces. But be careful—too much heat on large pieces of veneer will change the fit.

Petals are cut in one at a time. Crisp boundaries between individual petals in this sample piece enhance the image's three-dimensional feel.

head. First draw the outline of a bird's head on your background, and then inlay a beak into the background. Spread glue on the edges, and press the beak in from the back. Then make the cut for the head through the beak piece, giving a nice crisp edge where the head overlaps, as shown in the top photo.

Piercing involves drilling a tiny hole to slip the sawblade through. It's easiest to start all your cuts from an edge of the background, but inevitably, you'll have to drop a piece into the center of a background. Or you'll want to go back to add a piece after completing a design. That's where piercing comes in.

First I tape the pieces together. Then I use a tiny drill bit in a hand-held pin vise to pierce both veneers. Drill at one tip of the piece to be cut out (see the bottom left photo on the facing page). Release the blade from the top of your saw, and gently slip the blade through the hole in the underside of the bottom veneer. Reattach the blade, and cut out the design. This leaves a small hole in one corner of the pattern. It can be well-hidden with a mix of sawdust and glue.

Shading with hot sand

This last trick—sand shading—really adds depth and shadow to your design, as the flower in the photo at right shows. Wash some fairly fine sand, and heat it up on a hot plate. Pick up the inlay piece that needs a little shading with a pair of tweezers. Then dip an edge of the piece into the sand, as shown in the bottom left photo.

Check the inlay piece constantly because once the wood starts to toast, it darkens quickly. Be careful not to toast large pieces of veneer for too long because they have a tendency to shrink in the heat and distort the fit.

Finishing up

When your marquetry is finished, glue it down to a plywood core at least $\frac{1}{8}$ in. thick. And always glue veneer to the back of the core simultaneously to keep the stresses balanced and the core flat. I put a layer of cardboard on the marquetry and stack a few inches of particleboard on top when I clamp the veneer. Then I use as many clamps as I can fit.

After sanding, I finish with shellac because it doesn't distort the color of the wood too much. It's magic when you put on the first coat and the contrasts jump out at you. In this medium, you get textures, pores, colors and light reflections. That is really what makes marquetry so special. □

Gregg Zall is a woodworker living in Petaluma, Calif.

The Marquetry of Vadim Aksyeonov
An artist creates wooden renderings of Russian landmarks

by Jon Humboldt Gates

Despite the recent breakup of the Soviet Union and a declining economy in the region, the wealth of Russian art never diminishes. The marquetry of Vadim Aksyeonov is an impressive example of this wealth. Aksyeonov's wooden mosaics may be the most accomplished work of their kind to come from Russia. His proficiency as a painter is apparent; all his panels exhibit a remarkable three-dimensional quality (see the top photo on the facing page). In addition, Aksyeonov's work is of historical significance because some of the panels offer accurate representation of destroyed Russian landmarks.

Aksyeonov's formative years

Vadim Aksyeonov was born in the town of Menzelinsk, near the Ural mountains; from an early age, he dreamed of becoming a landscape oil painter. During World War II, while stationed in Lvov in the Ukraine, he sketched memorials and churchyards—scenes that would later inspire his marquetry. In 1955, Aksyeonov entered Moscow's Pedagogical Institute to study art and painting, and upon graduating, he became an art instructor. During this time, he often traveled to small villages to paint his favorite subjects: old churches and abandoned monasteries. In his free time, Aksyeonov taught himself the techniques of marquetry, and because his early works were translated directly from paintings, they displayed his characteristic treatments of perspective, light and shadow (see the bottom right photo on p. 78). In the 1980s, Aksyeonov began creating detailed architectural marquetry in tribute to Russian Orthodox and Islamic churches that were destroyed under Soviet authority. He also inlaid panels of old cityscapes, like the 18th-century Moscow Kremlin, shown in the bottom photo on the facing page. Working from photos and sketches, Aksyeonov recreated images of lost buildings by inlaying scores of native woods, like *beriozka* (birch), *kashtan* (walnut), and *klyoan* (maple).

Images preserved in wood

Aksyeonov begins his panels by drawing a subject (scaled by eye) with a pencil and a plastic straightedge. Then he transfers the drawing onto tracing paper so that he can reverse the tracing and copy it with carbon paper onto the back side of the veneers. Veneer samples are chosen for hue and grain pattern because Aksyeonov does not paint or dye any of them. He orients the veneer's grain and scribes the major elements of the scene onto them, such as the sky, foreground and buildings. After cutting out these large pieces with a knife that he crafted from a circular-sawblade tooth, he marks and cuts out the medium-sized elements from the larger pieces (see the photo above). Then he slides another wood variety under the hole and scribes the piece that will fit into the opening. He works from larger to smaller shapes, until all the pieces are cut.

Before mounting the veneers on a backboard of ¾-in.-thick particleboard or plywood, Aksyeonov uses sticky brown-paper tape to hold all the pieces together. He assembles the whole scene face up, and then cuts strips of tape, wets the glue side and presses the tape firmly over the whole surface of the scene. He smooths the taped joints with the butt of his knife's wooden handle. Next, he turns the taped-together sketch face down, spreads a thin, even coat of yellow glue onto the veneer back and the plywood backboard and places the glued surfaces together. To keep the assembly flat and the pressure uniform, Aksyeonov uses a 4-ft. by 6-ft. veneer press that's heated to about 150° by two ⅛-in.-thick zinc electric plates. The panel is sandwiched between two layers of newspaper, the zinc plates and two heavy wooden platens. The platens, which are larger than the panel and the plates, are pressed together, and the assembly is left to dry from 4 to 12 hours. After removing the panel from the press, Aksyeonov peels the brown tape from the surface, and scrapes off any dried glue. Next, he levels the veneers with a portable electric sander and hand-sands the surface to remove any scratches. Then he frames the panel and seals it with two coats of lacquer.

Current work

Vadim Aksyeonov, now 65 years old, continues to teach art and do marquetry during the evenings and weekends in the living room of his Moscow home. The panel he's working on in the photo above is his second attempt. When he was completing the scene the first time, his dog *Taiga* (Tundra) "ate it while his master wasn't looking." Every summer, Aksyeonov returns to Menzelinsk where he visits old friends, hunts in the forest, paints in the countryside and renews his creative energy for marquetry. ☐

Jon Humboldt Gates is a hobbyist woodworker, musician, and author of a collection of travel stories and photos titled Soviet Passage *(Moonstone Publishing, PO Box 911, Trinidad, Cal. 95570). Anyone wishing to arrange a gallery of Aksyeonov's marquetry, should contact Moonstone Publishing. Special thanks to journalist Oxana Khomenko for her research and translation help.*

From *Fine Woodworking* (May 1992) 94:62-64

Russian landscape painter and marquetarian, Vadim Aksyeonov, chooses highly figured woods for large elements, like the sky and foreground shown in this scene of the Church of Assumption at Pokrovka in Moscow. But he does most of the inlaying within the panel's building mass. This church was built from 1696 to 1699 and later demolished by the Soviets.

To create this image of Moscow's 18th-century Kremlin, Aksyeonov based every inlaid detail, including shadows, trees and reflections, on old sketches and photographs. The scene is an excellent example of the way Aksyeonov combines bold and subtle colors and grain.

This panel of Temple of Christ the Saviour (at left) contains hundreds of pieces cut from over a dozen varieties of wood from around the world. Built in Moscow in 1839 to 1880, the temple was razed in 1931. Church groups are now collecting funds to reconstruct the building at its former location across from the Kremlin.

Aksyeonov began his Myechet Church panel (below left) during an annual return trip to Menzelinsk. After its tower was destroyed in the 1930s, the building became a library until 1991 when it was returned to the Islamic faith, which is still popular in that region. The church, constructed in 1910, is currently having its tower rebuilt.

Exotic veneers are becoming increasingly difficult to locate in Russia. When he can, Aksyeonov uses native maple, walnut and birch, as in the panel (below right), completed in 1976, of Karilia's Peter and Paul Chapel near St. Petersburg.

Inlay Bandings Dress Up Your Work

Simple techniques produce intricate details

by Gary Straub

The simplest and most prevalent form of inlay is with strips of wood (bandings) as borders, but many woodworkers shy away from using inlay bandings, thinking it too difficult a process. Though some bandings can be time-consuming and difficult to make, many are not. Inlay bandings range from simple string inlay (a thin strip of contrasting wood) to exceedingly complex creations with hundreds of pieces comprising a geometric design. I'll discuss the basics of making bandings and then the specifics of a few different types (see the top photo on p. 80).

To understand the process of making bandings, you need to see the banding three-dimensionally. Bandings are not made individually but rather as a board that will be sliced into many identical strips (see the photo below). The simplest of bandings, a solid strip of wood, is perhaps the easiest way of getting a feel for making banding. To make 10 bandings for a large tabletop, I wouldn't just randomly select 10 thin pieces of wood. Instead, I'd select a board I liked and cut 10 consecutive strips from it. This way, each of the 10 bandings is virtually identical, and the grain pattern—however subtle—is repeated around the table. This technique is

the same for any type of banding. For strips that consist of more than one piece of wood, though, you have to make a board, and to do that, you have to know how big to make it.

Sizing the banding

First decide how wide to make the face of the banding. Commercially available bandings come in a myriad of widths, from less than 1/16 in. to well over an inch. The right width of banding will depend on the style and scale of your project. I always try to match a banding width to one of my router bits, so I can easily use my plunge router to make an accurate groove for the inlay. If you need a banding that doesn't correspond to any available bits, two passes with a smaller bit will give you any width you like.

Commercial bandings are 36 in. long, but I make mine to fit the piece I'm inlaying. I usually make the board a little longer than the shortest measurement of the piece. For example, for a tabletop 40 in. by 80 in. with banding 1½ in. from the edges, I'd make the banding about 38 in. long (40 in. less 1½ in. at either end is 37 in.). On something small, though, like a box top, I sometimes make the

Inlay bandings are sliced from a board that has been made for that purpose. Cutting bandings on the bandsaw results in less waste than cutting them on the tablesaw. It's also much safer on the bandsaw because there's no danger of kickback or of the blade binding.

An infinite variety of inlay bandings is possible. Your imagination is the only limit. As a rule, though, you should be sure borders of bandings consisting of a number of different woods contrast with the wood into which you're inlaying them. How these seven samples were each made is discussed in the text.

When gluing up straight from the saw, the author always uses the tablesaw outfitted with a good-quality finish blade.

Cutting laminations at an angle and combining them imaginatively give you a whole other range of possibilities for bandings.

banding as long as a side and an end combined. Of course, I often have to splice pieces together to get the length I need, but the idea is to create a length that neither falls just shy of a corner nor is so long that it's a pain to make.

The board's depth is determined by how many pieces you want to get out of it. Because I make only custom, one-of-a-kind furniture, I usually make the board just deep enough for the piece I am working on, plus a little extra in case of mistakes. To figure the depth, I add the thickness of the banding (I make mine ³⁄₃₂ in. thick) and the width of my bandsaw's kerf (¹⁄₁₆ in. for the ³⁄₈ in., 8 teeth-per-inch blade I use to resaw the bandings) and multiply that sum times the number of pieces I'll need, plus a couple of extras.

Designing and making banding

The next most simple type of banding after a plain strip of wood is a solid strip with a border of contrasting wood on each side (see samples 2 and 3 in the top photo). I resaw the three pieces to approximate thickness and then run them through the planer to exact thickness—a ½-in. center with ⅛-in. borders in the case of the two bands pictured. My planer goes down to ³⁄₃₂ in., so I don't need to rig up any special fixtures. Next I apply Titebond yellow glue and clamp the three pieces together with a thick board on each side to help distribute the clamping pressure. I use C-clamps set every 2 in.

A variation on this design, which looks more complicated than it is, is sample 5 in the top photo and in the photo on p. 79. Instead of using one wide center strip, I resawed and planed two thinner strips of walnut and used a piece of dyed veneer (available from most veneer suppliers) in the center. Then I drilled centered holes on the drill press and took a dowel smaller than the diameter of the drilled holes to spread glue inside each hole, one at a time. Finally, I hammered home dowels I'd sized exactly by forcing them through a drill-bit gauge's ¹⁹⁄₆₄-in. hole.

The geometric patterns in samples 6 and 7 in the top photo are similarly easy to make. There's just one more step in the process, and a visualization leap you have to take. I started by laminating three pieces each of maple and walnut, ½ in. by ¾ in. by 14 in. Then I jointed one side (of alternating maple and walnut) and planed the other to make them uniform after gluing. I cut the block into ½-in. strips at 45° across the grain (see the photo at left) on the tablesaw. I always use a tablesaw outfitted with a finish blade to cut pieces that will be glued up without surfacing. I used the resulting blocks to make banding 7 in the top photo.

There are a few tricks to working with diagonal pieces. To get

The author's wenge and mahogany shelving unit incorporates some of his own inlay banding, adding more visual interest.

length, you'll need to butt sections together. To do this, square up the end pieces, so you can more easily clamp the whole thing together lengthwise. Cut the two border pieces slightly shorter (⅛ in. or so) than the total length of the diagonal pieces. Apply yellow glue to the inside of both border pieces and to the juncture of every pair of diagonal strips. Clamp loosely across the width every few inches with C-clamps, and squeeze the diagonal pieces together with a bar or pipe clamp. Now tighten the C-clamps.

Strip 7 in the top photo on the facing page and the one I used in the shelving unit in the bottom right photo on the facing page was made using this same technique, except I cut the diagonal strips at ¼ in. and reversed them on top of each other, making a four-piece lamination instead of three. I also used plastic-resin glue instead of Titebond because it takes more time to set, which is helpful when you're gluing several pieces at once. Many banding designs are possible with this method, using the same building blocks (see the bottom left photo on the facing page). I made banding 4 in the

top photo on the facing page to create a similar look but without using a glued-up lamination. I used a piece of zebrawood that I cut on the diagonal, but this method will work with any wood that has prominent vertical stripes.

Sawing the bandings

Before cutting a board of banding into inlay strips, I first joint one edge, making sure it's square. Then I mark the top (perpendicular to the face) with a V to keep track of the order in which strips are cut. I cut the strips on my bandsaw (see the photo on p. 79). I prefer the bandsaw for cutting strips because there's less waste and because it's much safer than trying to cut the 3⁄32-in. strips against the fence on a tablesaw—an operation you shouldn't consider. After I've cut a board into bandings, I put rubber bands around the pack to keep them from distorting until I'm ready to use them. □

Gary Straub is a professional woodworker living in Columbia, Mo.

Preparing, cutting and inlaying bandings

A small miter box and a Japanese backsaw work well for cutting miters at corners and for splicing the banding. A Western-style backsaw also works just fine.

An inverted block plane with a very sharp blade is just the thing for shaving off tiny curls to get a piece of oversized banding to fit.

Inlaying bandings into a surface is only a matter of routing a groove the same width as the banding and gluing the banding in place. The tools needed are minimal, and the technique is basic.

The first thing I do is mark the corners where the outside edge of the bandings will go, so I'll know where to stop the router. The simplest way to do this is with a marking gauge. I use a gauge I've modified to accept an ordinary #2 pencil.

I chuck the correct router bit into my plunge router and set the depth of cut by using a drill bit ¼64 in. or ⅓32 in. narrower than the thickness of the banding as a gauge. Setting the router on a flat surface, I lower the router bit until it just touches the surface. Then I put the drill bit between the depth-adjustment rod and the stop post. I lower the rod snugly against the drill bit and lock the rod in place. This method is accurate and leaves the banding

just proud: It's easier to take off a little excess banding than it is to bring down the entire surface around the banding.

I put the edge guide on the router and set the distance using the marks that I penciled at each corner. Then I plug in the router and rout the groove all around, using my pencil marks as stop points.

If the banding goes in farther than my edge guide will allow, I use a Tru-Grip Clamp 'n' Tool guide (available in many woodworking catalogs) to guide my router. A straightedge and C-clamps also work. I determine where to place the guide by fastening it to a piece of scrapwood and routing a test groove. Then I measure from the edge of the groove to the guide to get my distance setting. Once I've routed the grooves, I square off the outside corners with a sharp chisel.

I start inlaying by cutting a miter on one piece (see the photo at left) and fitting it

into a groove with the mitered point touching the end of the groove. Next, if the piece extends past a corner at its other end, I mark where the next miter will be, indicate with a line the direction of the miter (so I don't cut it the wrong way) and I cut it. Then I put the mitered piece on top of the next piece to be cut, moving it around until I find a match. I mark it, cut it and continue to the next piece.

Where I need to splice pieces together for longer banding strips, I use either a butt joint or a miter, depending on the banding pattern. When inlaying bandings with geometric patterns, I sometimes reverse the pattern in the middle so that the corners will meet properly and be symmetrical.

If the banding is too tight for the groove, I just run it over a block plane mounted upside down in my vise (see the photo at right). If I need to take more than one pass, I alternate edges to keep the banding symmetrical. If I cut a piece too long or if a miter is slightly off, I use a sharp chisel to pare off a sliver.

Once I've cut and fit all the pieces, I glue them in. I use Titebond, only putting glue down for one piece at a time and making sure there are no dry spots. I force the banding down with the side of a round mallet, squeezing out any excess glue, always working from the middle out and pressing hard. After the last piece is in, I roll it all again. If the fit is good, the bandings do not need any clamping. By tapping my fingernail on the banding all the way around, I can find any spots where the banding isn't all the way down. Once the glue is set, I scrape off the excess glue and handplane the bandings flush with the surface using a finely tuned plane with a very sharp blade. Now the piece is ready for final sanding. —*G.S.*

Quilt Patterns in Parquetry

Scroll-sawing interchangeable pieces

by Charles Detweiler

My wife, Linda, and I launched a new career rather unexpectedly in 1982 when a recession in northern Texas caused a slump in our home-building business. With time on our hands and a need for income, Linda innocently suggested that we combine my interest in woodworking with her admiration of fabric quilts and make something to sell at a local arts-and-crafts show. After some prodding from our friends who sold at craft fairs regularly, we agreed to make some parquetry wall hangings based on traditional quilt patterns.

From that humble and hesitant beginning, our business has grown and prospered. Today, we make "wood quilts," the trademark we coined for the type of woodworking we do, in nearly 200 different designs and sell them to individuals, gift stores and galleries nationwide. Although the wall hangings are our largest sellers, we've also used quilts as tabletops, and we've grouped quilt blocks with different geometric and pictorial patterns into larger afghan-like works and montages. Recently, we've begun to sell wood-quilt kits, which have unpainted, pre-cut pieces that hobbyists can assemble, paint and frame themselves. But if someone wants a challenge and prefers to "quilt" from scratch, this article will show the fundamentals that we use to cut out and assemble a custom quilt.

Methods and materials

When most woodworkers hear the word parquetry, they think of floors decorated with geometric patterns. Our quilts are similar, in that small pieces of wood are cut out and glued to a substrate to form patterns. If only straight-sided geometric shapes, such as triangles, squares and parallelograms, are used, it's fairly easy to cut uniform, interchangeable pieces. You just rip strips of wood and then crosscut them into pieces at the proper lengths and angles. This method works fine and produces some beautiful patterns, but it limits you to straight-sided pieces. So in order to introduce curved pieces into our quilt designs, we developed a method for scroll-sawing the pieces.

Just as in conventional fabric quilting, most of our scroll-sawn wood quilts are based upon repeated block patterns, like the full-scale pattern in figure 1 on p. 84. Once we've sketched a block design, we decide how many times to repeat it to make up the quilt (we used 16 blocks for the quilts shown

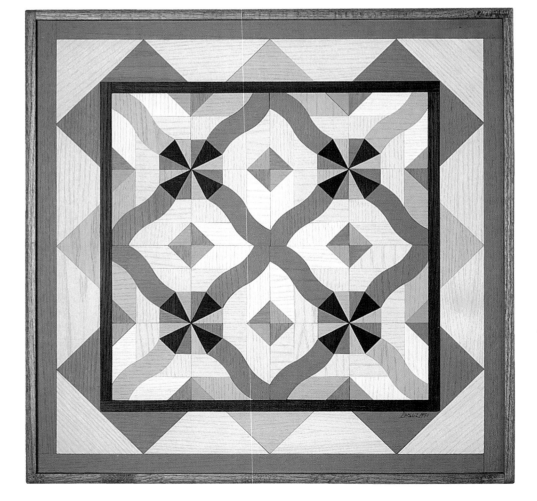

Dramatic design variations are possible simply by swapping colors within a pattern. The quilt shown above and the one at left have the exact same pattern, and even the same colors. A subtler variation is introduced when different kinds of plywood are used; the quilt at left is oak and the one above is lauan.

The 31-in.-sq. painted parquetry quilt, left, was inspired by a traditional quilt design. The quilt's field and borders are ¼-in.-thick plywood glued to a wafer-board substrate. Grain directions of the pieces were alternated to add texture and variety.

Photos this page: Susan Kahn

here). Then we cut squares—one for each block in the quilt—from ¼-in.-thick plywood. These squares are stacked in groups of four, the block pattern is drawn on the top squares and the stacks are sawn into pieces.

The beauty of this scroll-saw method is that we can use straight-sided, curved and irregular-shaped pieces, and they all have a well-matched fit in the finished quilt. Since multiple layers of plywood blocks are cut at one time, pieces shaped with arcs or free-hand curves are always uniform. Thus, various species of plywood can be used and the pieces interchanged, or the grain direction of adjacent pieces can be varied to introduce the look and texture of cloth. This scroll-saw method allows more design freedom, so I'll detail the process.

For a scroll-sawn quilt and borders, any species of ¼-in. plywood can be used. For example, in the bottom photo on the facing page, ¼-in. oak ply was used, while in the top photo on the facing page, ¼-in. lauan plywood was used. Thinner plywoods will be easier to cut, but they might be more trouble to glue and fit because they tend to warp. Solid wood can also be a problem, as the water from the glue can cause the pieces to swell and buckle or leave gaps when dry. We use ¼-in.-thick wafer board (available at most building-supply stores) for the back boards, though a thicker backing might be better if you're making a tabletop. All our scroll-sawn quilts are framed with solid oak and have ¾-in.-thick by 1⅛-in.-wide sub-frames, ripped from 1x12 white-pine boards, to stiffen the back boards (see figure 2 on the following page).

Although experience in making cloth quilts is helpful in laying out an original block design, you can find inspiration and traditional patterns in quilting magazines and books. By reversing color combinations of the pieces within each block or by rotating the blocks, you can achieve kaleidoscope-like variations. The quilts on the facing page illustrate the dramatic diversity possible by alternating colors and materials in identical blocks. Note that simple geometric shapes, like squares and diamonds, usually have common opposite- or adjacent-side lengths. By lining up equal sides, the shapes can be combined to make extraordinary schemes. Once you've arrived at a design, you can start to "quilt" your blocks.

Preparing plywood stacks

After you've selected the type of plywood, you're ready to cut out the squares that will later be scroll sawn into the pattern pieces. I rip 5-in.-wide strips on the tablesaw and then crosscut these into squares using a radial-arm saw and stop blocks.

Because the 16 squares will be arranged in four stacks of four squares each before they are cut into pieces, you need to draw your pattern on the four top squares only. There are several options for this: You can copy the pattern onto the plywood with carbon paper; you can cut a poster-board stencil with an X-Acto knife and trace it (see the top photo below); or if you are planning to make several quilts with the same pattern, you can make plywood marking jigs to trace the lines quickly and accurately; two or three jigs may be necessary to draw the whole quilt pattern. To make the jigs, cut single-pattern shapes out of plywood, and then tack and glue stops on two adjacent sides. These corner stops will align the jig on the plywood squares.

After you've transferred the pattern to the four top squares, you're ready to assemble the stacks with double-faced carpet tape, which is carried by most hardware stores. Place small pieces of tape on your design where you won't cut through them, because the glue on the tape will gum up the teeth of your scroll-saw blade. Since removing the tape is rather tedious, don't use any more than necessary. The placement of the tape will depend on the design, but don't put tape

on parts that will be snipped away early in the cutting process. However, at least two pieces of tape will be needed to hold the stack together until the last cut is made. To ensure that the tape is precisely placed each time, you can make a poster-board or paper stencil with windows cut out where you want the tape (see the top photo below).

When taping the squares together, alternate grain direction (two vertical and two horizontal), as this makes the quilt more visually interesting (unless you want a more homogeneous look). Also, align all the edges of the squares perfectly in each stack. It's a good idea to check this alignment with a combination square after the stack is taped together but before you cut. If the stacked squares are only out of alignment slightly (plus or minus ¹⁄₃₂ in.), you can belt-sand the edges flush since the glue-up procedure is somewhat forgiving of minor errors and since the frame can accommodate small discrepancies. When the taped-together stacks are aligned and square, you're ready to scroll-saw them into pieces.

Cutting and arranging the pattern

For sawing the plywood stacks into pattern pieces, I use a Hegner Multimax scroll saw

Poster-board patterns are used to trace the block design on the squares that will be on top of four stacks. Detweiler also cuts out stencils, like the one shown in the background at left, so he can precisely place double-faced tape between block layers, but away from lines to be cut.

By scroll-sawing four squares at once, Detweiler makes uniform pieces throughout a stack, allowing a piece to be exchanged with others directly above or below it. He uses a #5, 16½-t.p.i. Pebeco blade in his Hegner Multimax scroll saw (below).

(available from Advanced Machinery Imports Ltd., PO Box 312, New Castle, Del. 19720) fitted with a #5 Pebeco blade (also carried by Advanced Machinery). I prefer a #5 (0.0150-in.-thick by 0.039-in.-wide) blade with 16½ teeth per inch (t.p.i.) because it cuts smoothly and quickly and because it's stiff enough to cut sharp corners without much deflection. As you cut the stacks into pieces, set the pieces aside in the same positions as they were marked to keep things organized until the cutting is finished.

After cutting all the pieces, pry apart the taped parts carefully with a pocket knife or similar thin-edge tool, and peel off the tape.

If any of the tape's glue is left on the wood, clean it off with some paint thinner or alcohol. After removing the tape, the individual pieces within each stack are rearranged and laid out into new pattern blocks with the parts and grain alternated or rotated to complement the design (see the top photo on the facing page). Remember that all of the parts from one square will only interchange with others in that stack and only in the same place in the pattern. In other words, even if each square contains four similar triangles, each triangle should only be interchanged with others that are above or below it in the stack. This ensures that the pieces will fit

perfectly, even if you veered from the line slightly when cutting.

Borders

For first-time wood quilters, I recommend a single border, consisting of four equal-width strips around the quilt's sides. The strips can be whatever width you choose, but leave them ½ in. too long and trim the ends later. For the quilt described here, we used three borders. A ¾-in.-wide strip acts as a thin accent border to set off the block pattern. A 3-in.-wide border was cut into segments to form a pattern that complements the overall design. Segmented borders can consist of triangles or other geometric shapes determined by continuing joint lines and colors from the quilt's field. A little arithmetic will help you figure sizes. Finally, a 1¼-in.-wide outer border surrounds the exterior, like a mat. I recommend butting the joints of this outer border and the accent border, as opposed to mitering them, so that size adjustments can be made more easily.

Determine the length of the accent-border strips by compressing them around the field of pattern blocks lightly (four hands are required for this) and marking where each strip runs past its adjacent strip. Then I take the average length of the four strips and cut them all the same length by using a stop block on the radial-arm saw. I cut the segmented-border pieces by fitting them alongside the accent borders just established. I repeat this for the outer border, but I leave those ends long and trim them at the same time as the back board after the glue dries.

Now, cut out your ¼-in.-thick wafer-board substrate about ½ in. larger than the overall quilt size. This will allow for any block inconsistencies, accumulation of spaces between the pieces or out of squareness.

Painting the pieces

After all the components are cut, arrange the blocks and borders to make up the quilt on a smooth tabletop, and check that all the pieces fit well. Then spread out the arrangement, leaving space between the pieces so you can pick them up to color the wood. We brush on water-base liquid-acrylic paints, such as Accent brand (HPPG Borden, Accent Products Division, 300 E. Main St., Zurich, Ill. 60047) and Ceramcoat brand (Delta Technical Coatings, 2550 Pellissier Place, Whittier, Cal. 90601), which have a cream-like consistency and are available in 2-oz. jars at most craft-supply stores. We prefer these water-base paints for their ease in cleanup and overnight drying time, but you could also use household oil-base stains, enamel paints or thinned artist's oils; you should experiment on scraps first. Working with one color at a

Fig. 1: Full-scale block pattern

Sixteen plywood blocks are required for whole quilt.

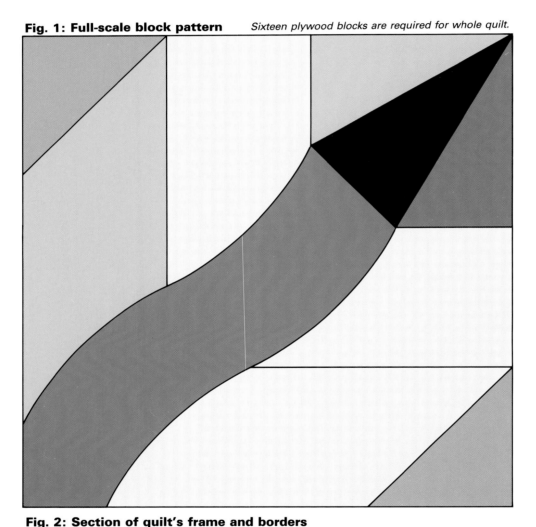

Fig. 2: Section of quilt's frame and borders

All borders and blocks are glued-and-painted plywood, ¼ in. thick.

Quilt field

Accent border, ¾ in. wide

Segmented border, 3 in. wide

Outer border, 1¼ in. wide

Finish nails, 1½ in. long, are driven into end of other frame members at corners.

Wafer-board back board, ¼ in.

Finish nails, 1 in. long, are tacked from back; three per piece.

Outside edge of frame stock is rounded over before frame is cut; corners are eased with a rasp after assembly.

White-pine stiffener, ¾ in. thick by 1⅛ in. wide

Stained oak frame, ¾ in. thick by 1⅝ in. wide, is face-nailed to stiffener with 1½-in.-long finish nails.

Photos except where noted: Jim Boesel; drawings: Aaron Azevedo

time, paint each piece and border, picking up and returning each to its designated spot in the layout. Spread the color evenly, brushing it in the direction of the grain. If you want the grain to be more apparent, apply a thinned wash coat of paint and immediately wipe it off to the degree of transparency you want. Let the painted components dry for 12 to 24 hours before gluing them to the back board.

Gluing and clamping

After the parts are dry, push the whole assembly snugly together again, but off to one side to make room for the back board. Next, mark the center of your back board, and from that point, calculate and measure where the outside edge of the accent border will be located. Clamp the accent strips in place, but don't glue them yet. With a carpenter's square, check that these strips form 90° corners. Span across the corners with strips of ½-in.-thick scrapwood, secured with spring clamps (see the bottom photo at right). Now you're ready to transfer the pieces that make up the quilt's field to the back board and glue them in place.

Starting in the clamped accent border's corner, spread a coat of glue (we use regular white glue) over just a portion of the back board, and then, working quickly, place the quilt's pieces; two people are needed to glue a quilt this size. When the field of pieces is laid out, clamp the other two accent strips to the back board to complete the far corner. Be sure you don't push the pieces and borders together too tightly or the assembly may buckle. Although the joints may spread a bit while the glue is drying, you can further exaggerate the space between the pieces to emphasize patterns and individual blocks. But work fairly rapidly so that you can make adjustments before the glue sets. (I use a water-filled spray bottle to wet the tops of the pieces to keep them flat and to lengthen the glue's setting time.)

After this inner assembly is dry, carefully fit and glue the accent-border strips and 3-in.-wide segmented-border pieces around the completed field. Finally, glue the 1¼-in. outer-border pieces at the perimeter. To prevent the border pieces from bowing, hold them down with scrapwood and spring clamps the same way you anchored the accent border when you began gluing the field. Leave the clamps on for approximately 60 to 90 minutes or until the glue has set, but hasn't completely dried. Then remove the clamps and scrapwood, and wipe down the surface with a clean, damp rag to remove any glue squeeze-out. To maintain flatness in plywood pieces, cover the assembly with a clean piece or two of Masonite or plywood, weighted evenly with 10 lbs. to 15 lbs. per

Pieces with different grain directions are interchanged to create texture in the overall quilt. First, the taped blocks are pried apart carefully with a knife. After the tape is removed, individual pieces are laid out into new pattern blocks. Note that all of the pieces of a stack are kept in their original positions in the pattern.

To keep the borders from bowing, they are secured with spring clamps and four, ½-in.-thick strips of scrapwood across the corners. The assembly is then covered with Masonite and weighted evenly with 10 lbs. to 15 lbs. per square foot while the glue dries.

square foot (we've used piles of books, stacks of plywood and paint buckets), and allow the assembly to dry overnight.

Framing and finishing

When the quilt is completely dry, trim the ¼ in. or so off the oversized back board even with the outer border's edges. We use a sliding crosscut box on the tablesaw to do this, but with a steady hand or a fence, you could use a bandsaw. For wall hangings, we glue and nail four, ¾-in.-thick by 1⅛-in.-wide white-pine stiffener boards around the perimeter on the underside of the back board (see figure 2) to help counteract the wafer board's tendency to bow as a result of the parquetry being glued on only one side.

If the quilt is going to be framed, round one edge of some long pieces of ¾-in.-thick by 1⅝-in.-wide frame stock using a ⅜-in. roundover bit in your router (this will be

your frame's outside top edge). We use oak frames, but you could use any hardwood. Prestain the frame stock, and crosscut the four pieces 1 in. longer than required. Butt the frame pieces around the quilt, and then glue and fasten them to the stiffener boards with finish nails (see figure 2). Trim the excess at each corner, and ease the sharp, outside corners with a rasp to match the rounded-over frame edges. Fill the frame's nail holes, touch up these spots and the corners with stain, and paint any blemishes in your quilt before applying the finish. With a clean rag, rub on a coat of thinned linseed oil (we use a 50/50 mix of oil and mineral spirits) to complete the quilt and frame. □

Charles Detweiler and his wife, Linda, make wood quilts in northern Texas. Their precut quilt kits are available through Detweiler Folk Arts, PO Box 2883, Sherman, Tex. 75091.

Inlaying Turquoise and Silver
Adding life and luster to ancient ironwood

by John S. Manuel

Larry Favorite stumbled onto the beginnings of his career as an artist and craftsman while exploring the Sonora Desert in Arizona. He found a piece of ironwood, one of the heaviest and hardest woods in the world, and brought it home. Nothing much happened with the wood until Favorite found himself out of work. Then, one day while walking in his backyard, wondering how he would make a living, he rediscovered his desert find. He had seen some crude ironwood vases and other items in a local craft shop, and decided he could make objects that were at least as good as those being sold downtown.

"The first piece I made was a letter opener," said Favorite, who now operates a woodworking studio in Greensboro, N.C. "I followed that with some small pieces of jewelry. I started buying silver cutouts from the Indians and gluing them onto the wood. One day a man asked me why I didn't do inlays."

Even though Favorite knew nothing about inlays, the man commissioned him to make a belt buckle with his name inlaid into it. Favorite figured out how to do it, but the job took a month. He's learned a lot about inlay in the 15 years since then, and he's won dozens of awards for his inlaid boxes, vases and sculptures, like those shown at left and on the bottom of the facing page.

Favorite works only in ironwood, which has a wavy grain pattern that varies in color from a maple-like pale cream to a dark mahogany-like brown. Favorite enhances its beauty by inlaying turquoise into checks and cracks; then he accents the wood with sawn silver in the shape of Indian dancers, trees, animals and even landscapes.

Collecting the wood—Favorite makes an annual wood expedition into the Sonora Desert, the only place in the world where his preferred type of ironwood grows. Favorite gets his wood from private property, but collects only dead wood, some of which has been lying on the desert floor for more than 1,000 years. Often the wood must be dug out of the sand, and Favorite

Favorite's award-winning boxes, right, and vases, left, are made of ironwood and inlaid with silver and turquoise. The lustrous finish comes from sanding with successively finer grits of paper and then buffing with polishing compound before applying paste wax.

From *Fine Woodworking* (July 1991) 89:56-58

The turquoise is pushed firmly into a crack with tweezers. After gluing the stone and then sanding it flush with the wood, Favorite repeats this procedure until all gaps are filled. Hairline cracks are then filled with cyanoacrylate adhesive and fine sawdust.

Favorite cuts out the inlay with a jeweler's fretsaw and a fine-tooth blade. A photocopied pattern of the inlay is glued to the silver sheet to guide the cut, and a jeweler's bird-mouth pin supports the thin metal as he makes the intricate cuts.

has often irritated a few rattlesnakes and even a Gila monster.

Ironwood weighs 80 lbs. to 90 lbs. per cubic foot; so the pieces must be cut into lengths of no more than a few feet before they can be carried or dragged. Favorite chainsaws the lengths, but because of the hardness of the wood itself and the sand in its pores, he ruins four to five cutting chains per trip. Before cutting, Favorite decides how the pieces will be used and what grain patterns should be preserved. A sinewy branch may be best suited for sculpture, a stump for a vase, a straight section of trunk for boxes.

Preparing stock—Because he likes to preserve the wood's natural growths and weather-worn shapes, Favorite does little cutting or shaping for vases and sculptures. After minimal shaping, these pieces are sanded and polished, as described on the following pages, before they are inlaid.

To make a box, however, Favorite bandsaws sections from the logs with a ¾-in.-wide, 10 teeth-per-in. (t.p.i.) blade. From each section, he cuts a slice about ¾ in. thick from the top and bottom, to make the lid and base of the box. Both base and lid are then ground flat with 40-grit paper on a 6-in. by 48-in. belt sander. Ironwood dust is highly toxic; so a good dust mask and adequate ventilation are essential here. Once ground flat, the pieces are set aside.

The next step is to cut out what will become the inside or hollow of the box. Switching to a ¼-in.-wide blade, Favorite bandsaws through one side of the body of the box and cuts out the center. A curved cut is easiest to make. He applies gap-filling cyanoacrylate to the sawkerf and clamps the entry kerf closed.

Once the glue has dried, Favorite smooths out the inside of the box with a 3-in. pneumatic drum sander. He starts with 40- or 60-grit paper, followed by 80-, 120-, 220-, 320-, 400- and 600-grit. Because the wood is tough, coarse sandpaper is important. Each level of sanding should just smooth out the marks of the previous level. "Once sandpaper loses its cutting ability," he says, "it tends to

burn or scorch the wood. Then when I've tried to finish the wood, I would get a rippling or orange-peel effect."

Next, the outside of the box or the vase form is sanded with 40-grit paper. Then, the vases and box components are sanded through 220-grit in preparation for the turquoise and silver inlays.

Inlaying turquoise—Many crafters consider cracked wood defective, but these flaws can be an advantage when inlaying. Turquoise fitted into these cracks and checks adds color to each piece and draws attention to the often beautiful patterns created as a tree dies.

Favorite buys blocks of reconstituted turquoise from Colbaugh Processing, Inc., So-Hi Estates, Box 209, Kingman, Ariz. 86401; 602-565-4650. He throws these blocks in a salvaged garbage disposal that he runs on his benchtop, plugging the inlet and outlet holes to contain the turquoise. The disposal produces everything from fine chips to marble-size pieces, making it pretty easy to find the size and shape piece to match the dimensions of the cracks and checks.

Before the turquoise can be inserted into the wood, splintered edges and other weak areas along the cracks must be smoothed with a flex-shaft or hand-held rotary grinder. Fine, carbide-tip dental burrs are best for this work. Donning a jeweler's loupe to magnify the cracks in the wood and the crushed stone, he uses a pair

of tweezers to select pieces of turquoise to fill the cracks. Each piece is pushed down until it is snug against the sides of the opening, as shown in the top, left photo on the previous page. At this stage, the turquoise may project slightly above the surface of the wood, but don't worry about it. Everything will be sanded flush later.

Once the fissure is filled with turquoise, "Hot Stuff" Super T cyanoacrylate glue, available from hobby shops and mail-order woodworking suppliers, is applied over the top and sides of the turquoise. After the glue cures for about a minute, the surface can be sanded with 120-grit paper, either by hand or mounted in a drum sander. Dust created by the sanding fills the hairline cracks between the turquoise. Check for gaps and, if necessary, repeat the procedures with finer pieces of turquoise until all cracks are completely full.

With some pieces, you may want to stop now, and just finish the

Favorite outlines the area to be inlaid with a fine burr, and then hogs out the waste in the middle with a larger bit. It requires a steady hand to maintain a depth of cut that will leave the silver just slightly below the surface of the wood.

The silver inlay is glued into the routed recess with a couple of drops of cyanoacrylate adhesive and then gently tapped into place. Do not overheat the silver when sanding or buffing the piece or it will expand and pop out.

object. Favorite generally prefers to decorate his pieces a little more by adding a silver inlay.

Inlaying silver—As with turquoise, the silver offsets the dark color of desert ironwood beautifully. Favorite also uses the silver inlays to highlight or offset a particular pattern of wood grain. For example, he may inlay a windswept silver tree amid swirling wood grains. "I will make up a silver design based on how the wood speaks to me," he says, although he is partial to desert scenes and Indian designs, in keeping with the area from which he harvests the wood.

Once Favorite has selected a design, he draws it, photocopies it and then cuts out the paper image, so it can be tacked onto an 18-gauge silver sheet with rubber cement or spray adhesive sold by art stores. The silver is then set on a standard jeweler's bird-mouth bench pin and cut out with a jeweler's fretsaw and either a 4/0 or 5/0 blade, as seen in the top photo at right on the previous page. (Polishing compounds, buffing wheels, silver and other jewelry equipment used by Favorite are available from Rio Grande Albuquerque, 6901 Washington N.E., Albuquerque, N.M. 87109; 800-545-6566.)

After cutting out the image, Favorite lays it on the wood and traces around the edge with a 0.5mm drafting pencil. He then removes the silver and carves out the inlay area with a Dremel Moto-Flex Tool and three different cutters. First, Favorite cuts just inside the pencil line with a #171L Midwest carbide burr, also available from Rio Grande Albuquerque. Holding the burr at an angle, he undercuts the line enough to fit the silver inlay just below the wood's surface. The undercut edge also forms a slight lip that helps hold the inlay in place. After the outline has been roughed out, Favorite goes around the recess with a small #169 burr, enlarging the border. Then, the middle of the recess is cleared out with a Dremel #650 ⅛-in.-dia. straight cutter (see the top photo). The small burrs used to outline the recesses—a #170 or #169—are also handy for cutting out minute features, such as the toe of a bear. Regardless of the shaping operation, sharp burrs and cutters are a must. Favorite constantly changes cutters; it usually takes less than a half hour of work to ruin a burr.

After putting a few drops of cyanoacrylate glue on the wood, Favorite taps the silver image in place with a small metal hammer, as shown in the bottom photo. He then sands the wood down to the level of the silver, starting with 220-grit and followed by 320-grit paper on a pneumatic sander with an 8-in. drum.

Finish-sanding and buffing—Once the wood is flush with the turquoise and silver inlays, Favorite repeatedly sands all surfaces with 400-, 600- and 800-grit paper using a small electric-powered finishing sander. "These sandings must be done very slowly and carefully, so I just barely contact the surface of the inlay," Favorite says. "If the silver gets hot, it will expand and pop up."

Vases and sculptures are now ready for final buffing with White Diamond Buffing Compound applied on an 8-in. buffing wheel turning at 3,450 RPM. Finally the piece is polished with paste wax to create a pleasant sheen and protect the wood surface.

Boxes are assembled before final buffing. This procedure is pretty simple. The bottom is attached to the body of the box with cyanoacrylate glue. Tops are usually secured with insert hinges fit into recesses cut in both the top and side of the box with a slot cutter chucked in a table-mounted router. The insert hinges (available from Woodworker's Supply of New Mexico, 5604 Alameda Place N.E., Albuquerque, N.M. 87113; 800-645-9292) have barbs that stick in the wood, but as added protection, Favorite puts a drop of cyanoacrylate into each slot before putting in the hinge. □

John Manuel is a freelance writer living in Durham, N.C. Larry Favorite can be contacted at Route 2, Box 198, Stokesdale, N.C. 27357.

Freehand Inlay
A cribbage board provides good practice

by Salvatore Pontecorvo

The author inlays a separate piece of veneer for each group of holes on his cribbage boards. He glues a photocopy of the pattern onto the board as a guide for mortising and to align the inlays in the S pattern. An identical photocopy is cut up, glued to small pieces of veneer and used for trimming the inlays. The moment of truth comes when the paper patterns are sanded off to reveal the finished board.

Most people are very impressed when they see perfectly fitted inlay on a piece of antique furniture. It's natural to assume that the craftsman who inset these small pieces of colorful veneer into a solid-wood surface had years of experience and labored over the final fit. But the truth is with the proper technique, a steady hand and a little practice, just about anyone can succeed at freehand inlay.

The cribbage board in the photo on p. 91 is a good first project for learning freehand inlay. By the time you've mortised the game board and cut and fitted the 24 separate pieces of veneer that make up the S-pattern, you'll either be quite accomplished at inlay or you'll know that it's not for you. The skills that you acquire on this practice piece can then be used to inlay any shape you wish.

My methods are simple: Glue identical patterns onto both the piece to be mortised and the inlay veneer; remove the waste from the mortise with a router and work to the edges with a chisel; cut out the inlays with a razor knife and glue them into the mortises; sand off the paper patterns and sand the inlays flush with the surface. For the cribbage board, drill the holes before sanding off the paper so that any tearout caused by the drill bit can be sanded away when flushing up the inlays. (Cribbage aficionados will note that the board in the photo has 120 holes, so a player only has to go from start to finish once to win.)

Preparations

I begin by making three or four copies of a pattern I've drawn, preferably using 20-lb. bond paper (the heavier paper handles better). It's important to make all copies at the same time and on the same machine because photocopies can vary slightly in size from machine to machine and from day to day and even from different times of day on the same machine. The advantage of doing it this way (over cutting the inlays and then scribing around them for the mortises) is that with a pattern such as I use, it's much easier to align the individual pieces. It's also a substantially faster technique.

The extra copy or copies are backups. In the unfortunate event that you sand through a piece of veneer, you can still save the project from the firewood pile by remortising and recutting the inlay, as long as you have an accurate pattern.

From *Fine Woodworking* (March 1992) 93:89-91

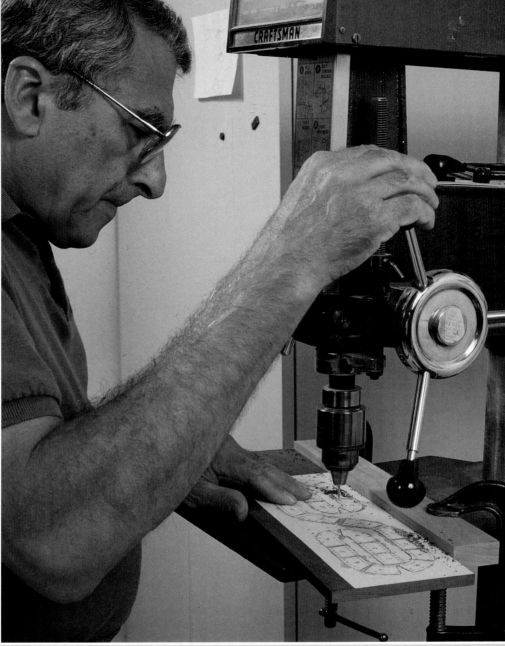

Routing the mortises rather than cleaning them out by hand saves time but more importantly, produces mortises of consistent depth with much less effort. The author takes the bit up to, but does not touch the incised line.

Trimming the veneer inlays to fit won't take long if the pattern lines are very fine and the cuts are accurate. Some will fit perfectly without any trimming; some will need just a little sanding; and some will require hairline cuts. A steady hand will save a lot of frustration later.

A fence clamped to the the drill-press table ensures alignment of the holes along the straight sections of the pattern. About two-thirds of the holes can be drilled using the fence; the remaining holes along the curves must be done freehand.

Once you've made your photocopies, the next step is to glue one of them to your previously thicknessed stock. I use a homemade PVC roller to get a thin, even coat of glue on the wood. After placing the paper pattern on the stock, use a dry roller to flatten the pattern. Make sure you've eliminated any air bubbles, and be careful not to roll the pattern excessively because that can stretch the paper. When the glue has dried, number each of the 24 segments on all photocopies. The numbers 6 and 9 should be underlined to alleviate confusion later.

Now, cut out each of the 24 paper segments—slightly oversize—from the second photocopy. Then glue each paper segment to a piece of veneer, also slightly oversize. I use veneers that are ¹⁄₂₈ in. thick. I don't recommend using thinner veneers because they are more difficult to work with than thicker veneers, and you're much more liable to sand through them. Again, use a thin

coat of glue between the paper pattern and the wood veneer. Allow overnight drying of glued patterns before proceeding.

Cutting mortises and fitting inlays

I use a sharp, #11 X-Acto blade to cut the outline of each playing-board section to be mortised. To ensure accurate cuts, I make the first cut with just enough pressure to cut through the paper and lightly score the wood, taking care to keep my cuts at 90° to the surface of the board. This creates a groove that will guide successive cuts of increasing pressure. I also cut each line from both ends to produce sharp corners. Cutting the lines deeper than the thickness of the veneer will make the removal of waste wood easier. The fit of each inlay will depend on how closely you followed the layout lines on the patterns, so go slowly and use care. Also, keep the knife blade sharp, and work with good lighting.

I clean out the majority of the mortise with a router and a single- or double-flute ⅛-in. up-spiral bit, adjusted to a depth just a hair thinner than the veneer. It's a bit risky having to sand or plane the veneers down to the stock, but it's a lot less time-consuming than the reverse. And though it's possible to use a larger diameter router bit, the ⅛-in. bit affords better control and allows a closer approach to the corners (see the top left photo on the facing page). Press one hand (or wrist) down tightly on the board, and use it as a pivot or anchor point for the router. This greatly reduces the risk of cutting beyond the lines. Let the router bit come as close to the lines as you're comfortable with, but don't touch the line. I first outline the perimeter of a section with the router bit, then move the router back and forth to clean the section out. It's important to go slowly at this stage, because a slip here will ruin the whole piece. Complete the final trimming of each mortise with a sharp paring chisel. (I use a ⅛-in. paring chisel because of the curves in the S-pattern, but a wider chisel could be used for the straight sides.) After you complete each section, pencil in its number for reference when inserting veneers later.

Trim each veneer inlay to size using an X-Acto knife (see the bottom left photo on p. 90). Cut the edges that run crossgrain first, and then cut with the grain. Pay close attention to grain direction, especially when cutting curves, and try not to cut diagonally into the grain or the veneer will split. As each inlay veneer is cut, test its fit to the mortise. Light sanding may be required to make the veneer fit properly. You're looking for a tight fit, not a forced fit.

Putting it all together

Once you've cut all 24 mortises and fitted the corresponding veneer sections, it's time to glue the sections in place. Any polyvinyl acetate (PVA) glue will work, but I like Elmer's Brown Carpenter's Glue because it blends better with darker woods. Brush a thin coat of glue into each mortise, and then insert the proper piece of veneer. When all 24 pieces are glued in place, set a sheet of wax paper over the game board, place another board on top and clamp the two together. Let the glue set overnight.

The next step is drilling the holes. For those that fall in a straight line, I clamp a guide board to the drill table (see the photo at left).

For holes on curves, I bore freehand using the pattern holes. It's considerably more difficult for the human eye to discern misalignment on curves than on a straight line. I use a ³⁄₃₂-in. bit and set the depth stop on my drill press to ¹⁄₁₆ in. less than the thickness of my stock. Using a sharp bit at a high speed produces crisp, clean holes.

Until now, all you've been looking at has been white paper with black lines—kind of like looking at the back of a tapestry and seeing only knots and loose thread. Now comes my favorite part of the project, as well as the moment of truth: sanding off the photocopied patterns (see the photo on p. 89). As the wood is gradually exposed, the beauty of the contrasting woods is revealed, along with the accuracy of your inlay work. I use a random-orbit or palm sander and begin with 60-grit sandpaper and work my way to 240-grit. I switch from the 60-grit to 120 as soon as I'm through the photocopy since the coarse sandpaper is quite aggressive in removing material. I try to sand only as much as is necessary to clean up the board. I also finish-sand the bottom of the playing board at this time.

Now that you have two finished surfaces, you can cut the playing board to size and rout a decorative edge bead if you like. At this point, the playing board is complete, but I prefer to use the board as a hinged top to a box. This provides storage space for the scoring pins as well as for a deck of playing cards (see the photo below).

I finish the boards and boxes with one coat of clear-lacquer sanding sealer brushed on. Tung oil makes a good substitute. After the lacquer or tung oil has dried, take 400- or 600-grit wet/dry paper and sand the finish to a silky state. A coat of hard wax (such as carnauba) can then be rubbed on and buffed to a glossy finish. ☐

Salvatore Pontecorvo is a retired engineer and has been an amateur woodworker since 1959. He lives in Fort Wayne, Ind.

Photo this page: Susan Kahn; all other photos: Vincent Laurence

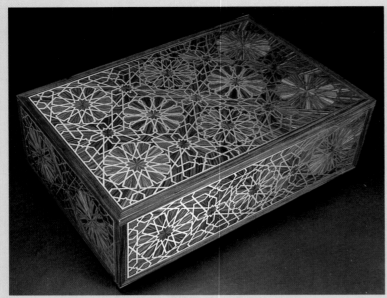

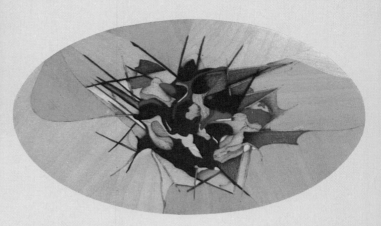

The design below is an example of the way some contemporary artisans employ ancient marquetry techniques to make attractive modern compositions. Despite the long tradition of marquetry around the world, today's practitioners contend that the decorative possibilities of the art form have not been exhausted, especially in light of plastics and other high-tech materials that are now available to marqueters. Made from multiple sheets of sycamore, amaranth, coral and satinwood, this elliptical casket represents an abstract design. It was designed and executed by students of the Ecole Boulle, and it is 9¼ in. high, 5½ in. wide and 3¾ in. deep. (Photo: J.P. Vial).

This inkstand box, which is approximately 6¾ in. high, 20 in. wide and 13¼ in. deep, is based on Islamic art (Alhambra Palace in Granada). Cut piece by piece, the marquetry is of kingwood and arranged as suns, and inlaid into a brass grill. The interior is from moiré satinwood and amaranth. The artisans who constructed the box carved their initials inside the cover.

Left: This fantasy subject, by an Ecole Boulle student, is made from barwood, blackened pearwood and blue-dyed sycamore. The flowers are from amaranth, the butterfly from boxwood, the tree from stained bird's-eye maple and the background from flecked sycamore tinted silver-gray. Using dyed veneers enables the marqueter to enrich the overall piece without necessarily increasing the decoration. (Photo: B. Novi). Right: Constructed in 1976, this stereo cabinet has marquetry motifs. Notice the contrasting darker and lighter veneers typical of the period.

Marquetry
Decorating with a palette of colored woods

by Pierre Ramond

Above: This 25½-in. by 24½-in. piece was created in classes on perspective and executed by Ecole Boulle students. The sky is Brazilian rosewood; the dam is tulipwood and amaranth; the skeleton is West Indian boxwood, Ceylonese satinwood and pearwood; and the rocky cliffs are figured mahogany, walnut and macassar ebony. The veneer is in natural colors. (Photo: B. Novi). Below: More evidence of dyed wood that was used in marquetry are these ceiling tiles, created by Michel Lefèvre, that are made from sycamore that's been stained silver-gray.

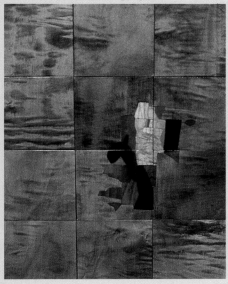

Most furniture made by contemporary designers was rather conventional, although it was enriched with beautiful marquetry. The coffee tables, shown above and below, represent rather unique, and somewhat abstract, designs. The original ideas and designs are by Luis Ansa, who was inspired by the Cubist School, and the marquetry is by Pierre Ramond. (Photos: Peter Shummer).

Marquetry is the art of painting with wood. Also called intarsia or inlay, it encompasses making pictures and geometric designs with thin slices of colored wood, shell and other precious materials. It is a popular technique for decorating the smooth surfaces of pieces of furniture, as well as a versatile means of creative expression.

The art of marquetry is ancient and dates back to marble incrustations in the palace of King Mausole in 350 B.C. For many centuries after that time, marquetry was centered in Paris, although English and German cabinetmakers were actively decorating furniture with marquetry as well.

In North America, marquetry was not as popular as in Europe. The decoration of 18th-century furniture was taken from the Eng-

lish and Colonial styles, but the shapes and designs were far less elaborate. Much of this early American marquetry was made by a constituent of cabinetmakers in Boston, Mass., who found wood plentiful in this country and worked with sculptors, gilders, turners, upholsterers and lumbermen to cut and prepare veneers.

Between 1788 and 1810, "Early Federal" furniture evolved, influenced by George Hepplewhite's and Thomas Sheraton's styles. The "Later Federal" period (1800-1840) boasted pieces veneered with light-color woods. Since many more European cabinetmakers settled in America during the mid-19th century and onward, some of the more popular European styles, such as Gothic, Rococo, Renaissance and Louis XIV, were very much in fashion in the United States.

In the years between the two World Wars, many cabinetmakers

The marquetry in the chest, right, was cut in veneer from "luxury" woods of exceptional quality: kingwood and rosewood from Madagascar, and brass. Like many marquetry pieces, this is an interpretation of a drawing. In keeping with the originality of the drawing by Cornelius Escher, the tracing silhouettes the figures the same way on the top and bottom and the reverse way in the center. This type of composition can be executed in the 17th-century technique of André-Charles Boulle, who developed compositions made from wood, shell and metal, cut in superimposition, and assembled in positive and negative. Here the rosewood is superimposed on the brass, and obtains identical patterns at the same time, but with the contrasts reversed. After the pieces of marquetry were veneered on the box, the details of the figures were engraved with a burin. The engraved figures are more visible on the brass.

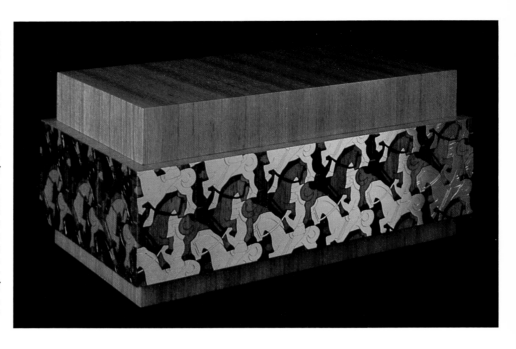

continued working and adopted the Art Deco style. Although the merit of the artistic taste during this period is questionable, the marquetry created was of a very high technical standard. In fact, to cut the very fine grill work that was essential to cloisonné motifs, experience and great manual dexterity were required. Works by Jacques-Emile Ruhlmann with their delicate ivory interlacing are proof of such skill. (For more on Ruhlmann's work, see *FWW* #51, pp. 35-37.)

While the aesthetic quality of the style may be disputed, the artisans were still able to craft superb copies, faithful to the ideals of their predecessors. Since the last century, there has been considerable mechanical progress: The workbench is in its most advanced form and the pedal or electric scroll saw is able to cut a number of veneers simultaneously, producing several copies of a marquetry motif. Many tools, including the small circular saw and trimmer, accelerated the use of marquetry and improved the precision of the arrangements, thereby lowering the cost by increasing the output.

The industrialization of recent years and the progressive disappearance of artisans, however, have discouraged the survival of marquetry. After World War II, furniture was made in mass, and marquetry was not frequently included. It was at this time that marquetry decoration was adapted in "Moustache" style furniture. The furniture made during this period was rectilinear and rather conventional, although it was enriched with beautiful veneer work. Cabinetmakers produced large quantities of furniture that was almost identical, but was covered with a different veneer, that was either dark (Indian rosewood or ebony) or blond (Baltic birch, bird's-eye maple or sycamore), the paleness of which was accentuated by applying hydrogen peroxide before varnishing.

Fretwork medallions were incorporated into doors of wardrobes and cupboards and on tabletops and headboards. The main part of this decoration was in speckled, moiré, marbled or flamed veneer, arranged simply or with a background effect, such as mosaic squares or circles. The frame was either pierced or fretwork and made from striped veneer of the same tonality, contrasted by a fillet that was 1mm or 2mm wide. This fillet was commonly made from boxwood or sycamore on a darkened-wood ground, or amaranth, ebony, pearwood or hornbeam stained black and inlaid into light furniture.

The elements of character—Wood is the most frequently used material in marquetry. Although a wide assortment of natural-color wood is available, an infinite variety of hues are also possible with dyed wood. Veneer manufacturers classify wood into three categories: exceptional-figured qualities, which includes walnut, elm, oak, tropical wood, nearly all mahogany, avodiré, makoré and teak; luxury wood, which includes tropical wood that provides veneer that is moiré, waved, speckled or flamed, as well as maple, European cherry, tulipwood, kingwood, rosewood, amaranth, satinwood and ebony; and common wood, which is used for plywood and industrial veneer, and includes poplar, beech and most of the species in the other categories if they don't contain any unusual characteristics. All wood veneers composing a marquetry are selected from exceptional-quality wood, usually from the luxury category.

However, it is not uncommon to see imitations. Plastic laminates with a wood design or geometric composition on reconstituted veneer are easily identified as false marquetry. But new techniques, like transferring, make the expert's task of recognizing a false marquetry piece even more difficult. This method consists in making a genuine motif in wood, which is cut out, and then inlaid by a marqueter. It can be photographed and reproduced, sometimes by the thousands. The photograph, printed on paper or vinyl, is glued onto the piece of furniture, and a coat of polyester or polyurethane varnish eliminates any trace of lamination. Stenciling is another method and involves decorating pieces of furniture with paint that commonly imitates boxwood, ebony, mother of pearl and copper bandings. When the work has been done carefully, stenciling is a fairly good and undetectable method of reproduction.

In recent years, the increasing use of plastic laminate and the popularity of lacquered furniture have seriously impacted the use of marquetry. Louis XV, Louis XVI and Charles X furniture has been in demand, and the use of marquetry in these pieces has been maintained. A few contemporary artisans have created modern compositions decorated with new and different materials. However, the true marquetry craft is so relatively unknown and the standards of craftsmanship have declined that the decorative possibilities offered by this art form are not fully utilized. □

Pierre Ramond is a teacher at l'Ecole Boulle, the University of Paris I and Paris IV and at the Sorbonne, as well as at the French Institute for the Restoration of Works of Art. This article has been adapted with permission from the new English-version book, Marquetry, *©1989, which was published jointly by Les Editions H. Vial and The Taunton Press.*

Index